Jan 5 1993.

Steve

I thought you may enjoy this. it made the best sellers list in the UK this Xmas. Thanks so much for introducing me to the game – promise I'll make it.

FROM THE WOOD TO THE TEES

Also by Tom O'Connor published by Robson Books

The World's Worst Jokes

FROM THE WOOD TO THE TEES

An Amusing Golf Companion

TOM O'CONNOR

Caddie: David Stuckey

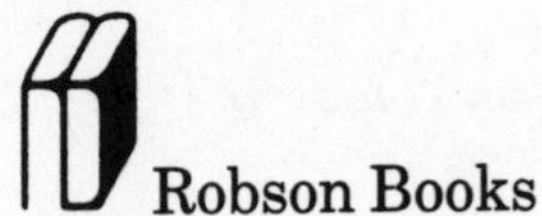

First published in Great Britain in 1992 by Robson Books Ltd, Bolsover House, 5-6 Clipstone Street, London W1P 7EB

British Library Cataloguing in Publication Data
A catalogue record for this book is available from the British Library

ISBN 0 86051 812 4

ILLUSTRATED BY JIM HUTCHINGS

Photoset in North Wales by Derek Doyle & Associates, Mold, Clwyd.
Printed and bound in Great Britain by
Butler & Tanner Ltd, Frome and London

Contents

THIS BOOK is dedicated to my lovely Pat, the best wife and roadie in the business.

All the stories are true. Only the names have been changed to protect the wrongly handicapped.

PROLOGUE

Teeing Off

GOLF IS the best of games, golf is the worst of games.

On a bad day, golf has a fury that would frighten Lucifer himself.

On a good day, golf has a serenity seemingly bestowed by the angels.

It has heights of ecstasy and lows of despair, and extreme swings of temperament such as are unknown to any other sport.

Golf is the last bastion of sportsmanship, fair play and competitiveness.

Golf is also wide open to abuse, score manipulation and law-breaking.

It has a language and a humour all its own – 'He's the type of golfer who shouts "Fore!", shoots six and puts down five on his card …' 'He's the only person I know with three balls in play and none is a provisional …'

Golf is played by using virtually every muscle and fibre in the body, but is governed by the six inches of grey matter between the ears. If you feel well, you play well, and the art of golf lies in preparing yourself to feel well – no matter what.

I have played well. I have played badly. And I've heard myself saying, 'Never again!' or 'What am I doing?' or maybe 'That's a worker!' – and similar choice phrases – time and again.

I have had pars and bogeys, eagles and birdies. I have broken 80, I've parred a course, but I've never reached the 'holy grail' of a hole in one (which, according to my mate Paul is only a 'fluke shot' anyway)!

In golf, if I can't claim to have been there and back, I reckon, like most incurable fanatics, to have been some of the way and enjoyed it.

Join me as I wander the course again, and remember …

My thanks to Mizuno, Stylo and Veldon Engineering for their unstinting support.

FIRST HOLE

When the Bug Bites

'WHEN THE bug bites, you never get free.' How true were the words of my first road manager Tommy, an ex-footballer, a great snooker player and a steady golfer. He used to tell me, 'I'm not very good, boss, but I'm hard to beat' – and he was!

In the summer of 1977 a wonderful man called George Willard told me, 'Remember, the golf club is a pendulum. She moves in a circle … remember our old friend the circle.'

George had in his time helped Val Doonican to become a single-figure golfer and given first lessons to a number of celebrities doing summer season. He also had limitless patience for the job.

And I was a wet-nosed comic from Liverpool, appearing twice nightly at the ABC Theatre in Great Yarmouth – and spending all day doing nothing, much to the chagrin of Tommy the Roadie.

'Boss,' he urged, 'come on! The sun is shining, the day is free. Just give it a try …' And like a school-kid taking his first drag on a surreptitious Woodbine behind the bike shed, I was led to the golf course – the ex-teacher going back to school.

How lucky I was that the teacher prepared to give me

my introduction to golf was George Willard, a gentleman, a pro and a stickler on the etiquette of the game.

An hour of chat and indifferent practice swings, not a little frustration and contemplation, and a good deal of listening and learning, culminated in my hitting a seven-iron shot that seemed never to come down – as a little old lady once said to me, 'It's the second best feeling in the whole world!'

George made me quit after that good shot. 'Remember, son,' he told me, 'it's the good one that brings you back.' And he was so right – the bug had bitten! I was never to be the same man again.

I bought my first clubs, with a bag and a trolley, and golf balls which retailed at 30p each – oh, how times have changed!

After three days of lessons, I was led to the tee for the first of six actual golf holes played. 'Just play the loop,' George suggested, 'where you won't be in anyone's way'.

A par on the third hole – two seven-irons and a 20 ft putt – and the world was my oyster.

A happy summer followed with more pars and surprisingly few disasters, with good habits taught by George and bad habits picked up from fellow golfers. Isn't it funny how you remember bad advice longer than good advice? …

On a long dog-leg hole, George would tell me, 'You'll take two shots to the green anyway, so hit a four-iron down the fairway and a five-iron to the green.' This worked more often than not and kept the blood pressure at a normal level.

At the same hole in the company of a fellow hacker, I heard: 'A big feller like you can open his shoulders and lamp one over the corner. You'll only be a wedge away from the green …' I swear that 'lamping' a ball over the corner of a dog-leg has cost me more balls than you'd need to furnish a driving range – but so what? When the bug bites, all sense disappears.

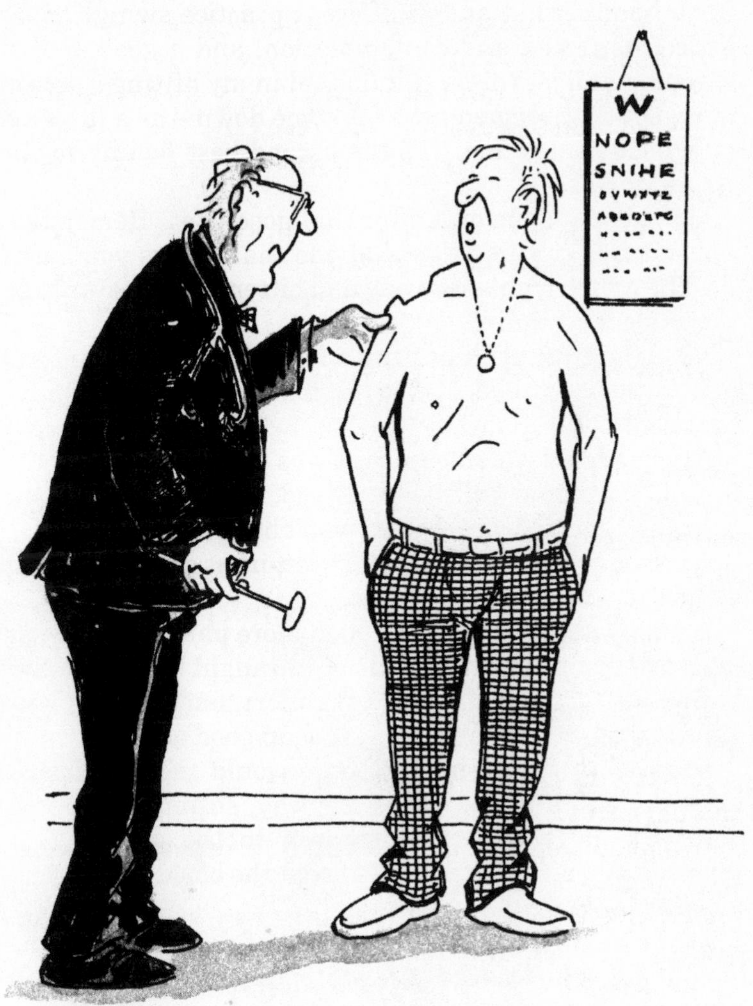

Golfer's shoulder

I have seen late nights pale into very early mornings, I have seen practice grounds with dew still on the grass, I have suffered blistered hands and shoulders sore from 'golfers' shoulder strap'.

When the bug bites you become a sucker for every little invention and gimmick on sale in the pro-shop: 'All-in-one tool for cleaning clubs, balls, shoes, trolley wheels – £7.50'.

'Pro tees, guaranteed never to break, cannot be lost – 50p for five' (but who would ever need more than one!).

'Golf bag accessories – towel, score card holder, drinks container ...'

There are special shoes, socks, gloves, different designs for dry weather, wet weather ... balls of different consistency – low trajectory, high trajectory ... 'What the heck – get a dozen of each!'

After four weeks of practice, performance and post-mortem, you're ready for new clubs ... 'These are all right for beginners but the way you're hitting them you need the new Sevvy Ballesteros set, like me!' So speaks a bloke who's been playing for 20 years and still can't beat me ...

But he must be right because he knows all the terminology ...

'I was two under fives for the first nine.' (What is he talking about?)

'We play five, five and five with oozalems and presses.' (Come again?)

Actually this is a accumulator game when you are playing for money and counting birdies – a deadly 'double or quits' cocktail which can be a surefire way to lose your mind – and a lot of money. I saw a man lose a Merc that way once – and, believe me – I definitely don't want to know!

Yet it is true that just when you think that golf is about playing for pleasure, about putting a small ball into a small hole, you are stunned to discover that the only sure test of skill lies in what you say.

How often have we stood on a tee and watched a player completely duff a shot, then heard ourselves say, 'That's a worker!' – just to rub it in. Nobody ever says, 'I'm going to hit a worker here.' Every shot tends to be a surprise – you're dumbfounded if it goes right, you're mortified if it goes astray.

I've seen a man hit a ball out of sand so fiercely that it cleared the green at a height of 60 feet and rising while his partner cried, 'Sit!!'

Perhaps my favourite all-time golf expression came from a pro-friend of mine, Alan Egford, who said, 'I've got this new driver – persimmon head, graphite shaft, 12 degree loft. It goes ten yards further than any other club I've ever thrown!'

Ah yes – the golf bug has many insidious symptoms and manifests itself by filling your head with dreams of greatness – 'If I'd only started younger, I'd be another Faldo …' It also covers your hands with calluses and fills your house with accoutrements you'd never heard of last year, and will probably never need next year.

The bug even affects the way you celebrate Christmas, miraculously changing all Yuletide presents from ties, hankies and socks to balls, tees, hip flasks, all kinds of golfing gimmicks …

The bug bit me in 1977 and I have not been the same man since. Despite everything, I reckon I have a lot to be thankful for.

SECOND HOLE

Keep Taking the Lessons

'REMEMBER son, that golf, particularly the swing, is very much an individual thing …'

Nobody needs to show you how to drink a pint of lager – it's natural. But just try to explain in words the exact movements your body makes in doing it … you can make even the most natural and seemingly easy task sound unnecessarily convoluted and complicated.

So it is with golf: 'I can explain the grip, the set-up, the balance, the swing, the follow through. But in those critical moments of doing it, you're on your own, pal!'

Good advice and good grounding from Nick Lunn, one-time resident pro at Lavender Park golf range, Ascot. Nick, a man always concerned with the right things about golf, was the first to get me to practise in front of a mirror to see the full extent of the swing and the plane ('think of a cartwheel!') and the high finish.

He was a man who succeeded in giving credence to the efforts of many a hacker by patience and care, a man who could produce a gentle draw shot from people who I'd swear did not know how they did it even after they'd achieved it. No wonder Nick, who had that happy knack of getting the best out of other people and making them feel really good about it, has moved on to golf

Practice in front of a mirror

management, organisation and public relations.

As well as the pros and those born to teach, I've learnt important lessons from some of the greatest, from those born to play. Stars like Lee Trevino, who told me once, 'Tommy (why do Americans insist on calling me Tommy?) if you wake up with a slice, play to a slice … and most importantly, Tommy, if it ain't broke, don't fix it.'

And Sandy Lyle added, 'Try to slow your swing down to a blur …' I knew what he meant!

Then there was John Jacobs, the ex-Ryder Cup player and one of the best golf coaches around – a real golfing master. He can give lessons to any golfer and, merely by suggesting small refinements, improve any game in an afternoon. John would tell me, for instance, 'There is a club in the bag for every shot. The driver is the only club you need to hit as hard as you can.'

On the practice ground one afternoon he showed me several things I was doing wrong and suggested simple remedies. Then I went out and had a round of golf with him – and beat him. As he handed over the fiver I won off him at the end of that round, he grinned, 'You wouldn't have won that without my help!' And he was right – I still have that fiver framed in my den.

So we've established that golf is there to be taught – although lessons seem to have a long-term wrecking effect on one's playing. Perhaps the best thing is to practise for six months but never actually to play. That at least would establish your natural game and 'groove in' the good habits.

After all, we all know how to play golf like Nicklaus and as long as we don't have to show we know, there's no problem. But golf is not like that – you can fool everybody except yourself and a good pro – 'If you swing like that and you say your handicap is 14, you must be the world's best putter, mate!'

Why can't we resemble computers and remember all

the good advice while forgetting all the useless stuff that's flying about? Computers have information punched into them – maybe they should punch it into us! Mind you, computers are also susceptible to bugs ... perhaps nobody or nothing is perfect after all!

I know from my days as a schoolmaster that good teachers give you two or three things to concentrate on, without confusing you with too much too soon.

So it is with golf. Concentrate on the set-up. 'Imagine an aircraft carrier,' I was told. 'A solid base made by the feet, the whole upper body pivoting on this, the arms and hands and club-head moving as one through the ball.'

An aircraft carrier? Yes – think about it. Anyone can land a plane on a runway. But try doing it when the runway is pitching and rolling, or even gently moving up and down. The art lies in the guy on the bridge keeping the *Ark Royal* as level as possible to aid the other guy trying to land the plane.

The take away: should be slow, deliberate – watch the shoulder go under the chin.

The follow through: our old friend the circle again! Maintain the swing and follow your hands through to watch the flight.

The head: down or up or whatever, the head should always be still.

The grip: too strong or too weak, watch the knuckles, the overlap, try it baseball style ... whatever!

Most important, don't try to remember everything at once. Just like the man told to put his best foot forward, shoulder to the wheel, head up, chest out ... you too could end up looking like Quasimodo and possibly suffering from 'golfers' droop', for which there is no known apothecary's cure.

The best lessons I have ever had consisted of 30 minutes on the practice ground followed by nine holes with the pro to experience real life situations – slopes, hanging lies, sand traps, trees, and so on.

And sometimes you can learn just by watching other golfers …

Trevino showed me an escape from under trees: take a six-iron, ball well back in the stance, a steady swing and the ball flies low and long. It looks good and feels even better if you call the shot before you play it.

Mike Burton, a great comic and a pal since our days together on *The Comedians*, showed me a wonderful sand shot: stance wide open, face wide open, swing out to in. The ball flies up and slices – a truly spectacular recovery shot!

Gil Dova, a brilliant juggler and a six-handicapper, on the first hole on the Burma Road, all of 472 yards and a par four, told me, 'Tommy, call it a par five and try to birdie it.' It certainly saved the grey matter worrying about whether to 'lamp' it.

John Jacobs even taught me how to plan a hole backwards. It's no use smashing a ball as far as possible, leaving an indeterminate shot with the wedge. Better a controlled drive, possibly a three-wood, leaving a full wedge or a nine-iron to the green. I sometimes wish I knew half of what John knows – or even a tenth of what he's forgotten.

Stories of golf lessons and golf advice are legion. My all-time favourite golf lessons must be the ones given by Alan Egford, then resident pro at Torquay. Alan was the first pro I knew who used a video camera to demonstrate the rights and wrongs of swinging a club. Believe me, it's more effective than listening to comments like, 'You're still trying to hit from the top, you twit!'

Unfortunately, the funniest thing that happened to Alan happened on the day his video was on the blink. But just picture it … 10.30 a.m. on a bright sunny June morning and into the car park at Torquay Golf Club

Mr Pale Blue swung

glides a pale blue Rolls Royce driven by a man in pale blue trousers, hat, shirt, socks. As he emerges from the car it is apparent that he also owns a pale blue golf bag with matching tees, towel, head covers and trolley.

Mr Pale Blue is in fact a scrap metal dealer, digital watch, sovereign ring, tattoos ('Love', 'Hate', 'Mum' and so on) – and he confesses to 'problems wiv me middle irons'.

On the practice ground with a six-iron, Alan ascertains that the problem lies in his swaying instead of turning his body in text-book style round the central pivot of his trunk.

Many, many efforts later and 'We are still swaying ...' So Alan says it is time to concentrate on 'keeping our head still while we swing around it' and suggests, 'Let's pretend that the head is fastened by barbed wire to the nether regions – then it shouldn't move.' But still it doesn't stop Mr Pale Blue swaying.

In desperation Alan comes up with a possible solution. 'Look,' he says, 'I'll hold your head in my hands while you swing' – and if the video had been working, what happens next could have become a Jeremy Beadle *You've Been Framed!* classic!

With Alan's hand firmly gripping the man's head, Mr Pale Blue swings – and while the whole of his body sways to the right, his wig stays in Alan's hand! The head goes out, the club completes its swing and the head returns to the wig.

Oh, the fun the pros must have at our expense when they gather together ... 'He'd be all right if he could get it in the air ...' 'He asked me how to play a putt on the 18th. I told him to try and keep it low ...' 'He's not the worst pupil I've ever had, but I can't remember who was ...' and so on.

My undying memory of the ultimate 'harassed' teacher was an American pro I met on the QE2. He sat at the golf nets all day, tumbler of gin and tonic by his side, a carton of Lucky Strikes, and his back to the 'pupil'. From that relaxed position he would shout, 'Too close to the ball' or 'Swinging in to out' or 'Swaying ... moved your head' or 'Breaking your wrists' – and the amazing thing was, he'd be right every time!

But then it is true – you too can 'hear' a bad swing. On the course it is accompanied by 'Oh no ...' or 'What am I doing?' or 'Aaargh!' or even '*!@÷△*f*≈œ*'

Memorable shots, holes, scores, days ... they're all a part of the rich tapestry that is the great game of golf. They are often things that only fellow golfers can share, moments that mean nothing to mere mortals ignorant of the finer art.

But more of this when we play 'The Game'.

THIRD HOLE

Playing the Game

IT'S THE GAME to beat all games, more attractive than any other to play, more religious than Sunday morning, more rewarding to play well, more punishing to play badly.

It arouses peaks of passion – I've seen rounds of drinks, and I've seen clubs round trees ...

There is the story of the golfer who has butted a tree a dozen times in rage. As his head streams with blood, he is borne off the course on a stretcher, and still manages to call out to his playing partners, 'Same time next week, chaps?'

Golfers are said to be eternal pessimists – witness the man who walked on to the first tee, took a practice swing, tore his card up and went home.

Or again, witness the man who topped his drive, threw the driver down the fairway in disgust, walked after it, picked it up – and threw it again.

There is many a home truth spoken in jest. 'My best two shots are the practice swing and the conceded putt', 'What goes putt, putt, putt? Me!', 'I started well, then he threw at 91 at me ...', 'I started 8, 8, 9, 8, then blew up ...', 'The most difficult wood in my bag is the pencil'.

Being not so much a comedian as a reporter of life, I

Playing the Game

have had a great deal of fun playing 'The Game'. I have seen triumph, disaster, heartache, ecstasy – sometimes all on the same day!

And one lesson I have learnt, sometimes the hard way, is that in golf, if they give you anything, take it!

I couldn't believe it to begin with, but it's true. If they say this is a preferred lie, if it's winter conditions and you can put the ball where you like – do it. I used to think this was a little like cheating. I wanted to be a good golfer and I wanted to be able to hit myself out of trouble, to play from any position.

Rubbish – at the end of the day the important thing is to get your ball out of the trouble and drop it somewhere. If they say it's a rabbit scraping and you're allowed a free drop, take it – because this guy won't be here tomorrow when you're trying to win his money and you're saying to no one in particular: 'Aren't I good – I played out of this hole!'

If you're murdering your opponent, if you've been given ten shots and you're knocking the stuffing out of them, don't say: 'I tell you what – don't give me any more shots. I'm playing well today.' Take 'em – drill the guy down, or as they say in Liverpool: 'Nail his hat on!'

Jimmy Mac is a big man, a builder, a Scouser and a steady ten handicapper.

I met Jimmy one Sunday morning at Childwall golf club in Liverpool. He helped me make up a four with two 18-handicappers, whose names should have been 'Butch' and 'Sundance'. Despite their obvious single figure ability, Jimmy and I had them neatly under control and were three up with three to play.

As he mounted the 16th tee, I said to Jimmy: 'We've got them. Now let's give them the *coup de grâce*.'

Jimmy shot me a withering look and said: 'Give them nothing!'

The game produces characters both good and bad. I've met the celebrity who had a pocket full of balls all the same number – the only man who never loses a ball in the trees but always finds it teed up with a clear sight of the green.

I've also met the man who by rights should be the author of the book *101 Ways to Improve Your Lie*, and the player whose pencil won't write more than five no matter what he scores. But then they are all part of golf's rich tapestry.

Why is golf the only reason men will let you leave a bar at night? You can say, 'I'm not well' and they say, 'Sit down. You look all right …' Or 'I'm working tomorrow' and they'll say, 'Calm down, there's stacks of time.' Or you try, 'The wife's not well' and they say, 'You'll only be another 20 minutes.' Tell them you're on tablets and they'll say, 'This'll help to wash them down.'

But say, 'I must go. I'm on the first tee at eight in the morning' and watch them sympathise. 'You'd better get an early night then …'

The game is all, and all about the game is memorable. Bob Scholes is an estate agent, a golfer and the only partner I've come close to strangling on more than one occasion. He has a habit of saying, 'Take it away' (meaning the flag), but it has resulted in many an opponent saying, 'Thank you' and picking up his ball thinking we've conceded the hole.

We were nip and tuck with a pair at Waterlooville. Bob was in trouble but I had driven to the edge of the green on a short par four. They were both out of bounds with their first drives, but one reached the green with his second and lay there for three.

As we approached the green, Bob opened his big mouth and said casually to our adversary, 'You're not going to putt that, are you?' He meant it as a joke, I suppose, but our surprised opponent said, 'No. Thank you very much' and picked up his ball for a conceded shot. That left me in rage to four putt, lose the hole and chase Bob nearly to the club house.

In my short golfing life span I suppose I must have tried every technique and every plastic-coated invention that's ever been produced to help me to play better.

It always amazes me whenever I play in a big Pro-Celeb-Am or the like that the pros don't have any of these things – the portable ballwasher, the combined score card, tee holder, pitch market, pencil and nail for taking things out of horses' hooves, the plastic-coated towel which never gets wet because it disappears up its own handle when not in use, the natty golf trolleys, motorised or transistorised or whatever, or the trolleys combined with bags that fold up to nothing and stack in the hold of an aeroplane ... all of them wonders that make up the wonderful world of golfing gismos.

Golf doesn't finish on the 18th green. It only just begins ... because that is when you go into the clubhouse and waffle on about your previous 18-hole exploits, or you go into the pro-shop and find out what else is new, the latest colour of sweater or golf shirt or glove, and thrill to the knowledge of the latest development. I'll never forget the first time I found out that FootJoy actually make golf gloves and gauge them by the size of your shoe. I couldn't believe it when the pro asked, 'What size shoe are you?' I said, 'Nine' and he said, 'This is the glove for you ...' and it was! Whether that was a fluke or not I still don't know ...

There are various implements to help you around the golf course – like the one for getting the ball out of the water. It looks like a ping-pong ball net at the end of a very long shaft, and it extends to scoop the ball out. There's the 'chipmaster club' which is basically a putter with a six- or seven-iron face. You take it away from the ball as a putter but when it strikes the ball it chips it, lifts it a foot or so off the floor and scuttles it along – a lovely pitch and run club for just off the green.

In my local golf club I have seen a driver which is actually supposed to correct a slice. In actual fact it looks like the rear light of a bike. It costs about £600 and if you slice the ball as you hit it, this thing corrects the slice and hits it straight – which is fine except that it only corrects the drive. What you do if you slice your second shot, heaven only knows. Unless you are going to buy an alternative set of clubs to correct your slice all round the course, the odds are you are bound to slice with your wedge even though the 'super club' has corrected your drive.

I have seen clubs made totally of titanium, fashioned all in one piece and costing about £950 . I've seen any number of weird and wonderful implements, all well worth the money, of course ... but when it comes down to it, what does it matter? If you can't project the ball correctly in the air and send it forward in a specific line, give or take the odd yard, what is the point of having a fortune's worth of equipment?

At the end of the day, for a learner, a good half set of clubs – a three-, five-, seven-iron, maybe a wedge, possibly one or two woods, and a putter is all you need. The better you get, the better is the equipment you can buy.

It is always wise to know when to speak and when to stay silent on a golf course, as we have already seen, and this is certainly true where equipment is concerned. One of my more embarrassing moments cropped up when I went to Anglia TV to prepare for a new game show called *The Zodiac Game*. I'd been told that the hierarchy at the station had a great love of golf and I was asked to make up a four with the producer, the programme controller and the head of light entertainment (otherwise known as God!).

The day dawned that we met on the first tee at Royal Norwich and to lighten the mood I decided to crash in with a funny. 'Have you heard,' said I, 'about the bloke on the first tee who said, "If anyone's interested, I'm playing a Commando 3", and his partner replied, "If you're playing a Commando, we don't need to know the number ..." '

As I laughed, I realised God was unwrapping his own Commando 3! Fortunately, he and the others saw the funny side of it and the show still went on.

Frank Carson woke me once with a story about the hard-pressed hacker whose bogey hole was the 14th – a par three, 167 yards, pond in front of the green. Every Sunday he planted one, two, sometimes three balls in the water and he'd had enough.

The resident pro recommended a prayer. 'I don't believe in God,' said the hacker.

'Well, you've tried effing and blinding. You've nothing to lose,' the pro told him.

So there he was on the 14th tee, three under his handicap, ball teed up and ready to go. And found himself muttering, 'If there is a God up there, will you help me?'

'Certainly my son,' said God. 'But first put away your four-iron and get out a three wood. You're playing into the wind.' And he did as he was told.

'Secondly, my child,' said God, 'you've teed up the ball too high. Lower it.' And again he did as he was told.

'While you're at it,' God added, 'that ball has more smiles than a clown. Use a different one.' Then as the hacker started to unpeel a Titleist, God said, 'Not a new one, you prat!'

Sometimes God's help may not be enough. Take the story I was told at the lovely Slaley Hall golf course just outside Newcastle.

That district was blessed with its own version of Mr Pale Blue of Torquay – but this man's problem was a

He swung it as he had seen the dustbin men do

massive hook. Every shot went left, all the time, sometimes like a batsman's pull to square leg. No amount of corrective therapy could cure this fault – opening the stance, weakening the grip, playing underwater – until it became obvious that our man was letting go of the club with his right hand, thus causing the left to pull everything round.

It was clear that the only cure was rhythm, or at least some means of co-ordinating grace, tempo and a firm grip on the club. The pupil was instructed to watch other people's rhythms – kids on swings, ballet dancers, tennis players – anything to try to find that elusive flow.

He found it while watching a bin lorry pull up outside Curry's electrical shop and seeing a dustman swinging bins on to the truck.

Having begged, pleaded and eventually bribed permission, he proceeded to attempt a rhythmic practice swing. He picked up a dustbin, aimed it at the cart, swung as he had seen the dustbinmen do, let go with his right hand – and hooked it through Curry's window! Oh, I do hope that story is true!

The game is all, and it's all about the game I write.

When all else fails, who can I turn to? Of course – I can turn to the caddie.

FOURTH HOLE

The Curse of the Caddies

THE CADDIES … ah yes, the caddies. Where would we be without them? Languishing in the rough, among the trees, deep in the bunkers without their advice, encouragement, side bets …

The caddies are living legends as famous in their own way as the pros. I've met many and enjoyed their company, their banter and their idiosyncrasies.

For two or three years running I played in the Howard Keel Classic at Mere Golf Club, Manchester and there I came across Ben, a man whose grip of the English language was constantly slipping.

Ask him, 'How's this putt, Ben?' and he would say, 'Straight as a whistle!' (Pardon?)

Ask him, 'What are you drinking Ben?' and he would insist, 'No, I'll get these. I'm in the boat.' (What?)

Ask him, 'What colour are your shoes, Ben?' and he'd say, 'Jet white!' (Come again?)

My first meeting with a real caddie as opposed to a mate who humped my bag, was in Southport. Drinking in the Fisherman's Rest pub, I made the acquaintance of the legendary Alfie Fyldes, caddie to Player, Watson and others. Alfie's knowledge of courses was unrivalled –

yardages, traps, wind directions – would he ever caddy for me?

'As soon as you get a swing, lad,' he said – and he was right.

Alfie and his brother Albert had me in absolute hysterics with their tales. Albert had a stammer and apparently when Alfie first got him a job as a caddie he was teamed with a player who suffered from the same defect. They were asked before the competition, 'Name your ball' and neither of them could say 'Titleist'!

I had only recently moved into a house backing on to Royal Birkdale golf course just outside Southport, and we were enjoying a few drinks in a local hostelry. 'How big is your lounge?' Alfie asked me. I told him and he said, 'I've got just the Persian carpet for you!'

We agreed a price and they promised to deliver it when the pub closed. It was one of those occasions when, your judgement clouded by the devil's brew, everything makes perfect sense …

So it was that at closing time, late night Southport revellers were treated to the sight of three grown men, the worse for wear, carrying a 40 ft by 30 ft Persian carpet from one side of the town to the other.

'Dog-leg here, Albert,' Alfie would shout as we turned a corner. 'Sh-sh-shut up. I-I-I can see …' he'd reply. I still laugh at the memory of that crazy night – and they are still my friends.

Scotland, bonnie Scotland, home of golf, the greatest courses and the ultimate in unique caddies.

It was pro-celebrity golf time on television, filmed at Turnberry, and I was to partner Sandy Lyle against Lee Trevino and Jimmy Tarbuck – very illustrious company.

To soften the blow of my first television golf appearance, it was suggested I play a practice round the day before to get accustomed to the nine holes, and introduce myself to Willie.

Now Willie (or 'Wullie' – where are you now?) was the archetypal Scottish caddie – purple nose, red cheeks, whites of the eyes brown, breath like kerosene, and an expert on the course.

I was with Kevin Keegan and a couple of friends, and a par three loomed, 157 yards, wind of gale force directly behind.

'Eight-iron, Willie,' I said.

'Seven,' came the reply.

'No, eight in this wind,' I insisted.

'Tack ma wurd, it's a seven.'

So I did – and I hit the ball with a seven. It was still climbing as it cleared the green.

'Well,' said Willie, 'it'll be a seven tomorrow ...'

On another occasion, Rover Cars arranged a special corporate day and flew 14 top dealers and fleet buyers up to Scotland for a day's golf. First class air fares, hotel, all you can eat and caddies paid for. However, there was a small request: 'We thought it would be nice,' the party was told, 'if you clubbed together to bung the caddies a tip.'

'Nobody bungs me and I refuse to tip my caddie,' said a portly gent, who arrived in a Bentley and had a watch like Big Ben. 'I prefer to hire a trolley.'

And this he did for the princely sum of £2.

The day dawned and we all trooped off down to the first tee, five teams of three, including me. The portly gent's team teed off from the second and as they proceeded down the fairway, three players, two caddies and a trolley, one player asked: 'What is it for me from here, caddie?' 'A five-iron, sir,' came the reply.

And the portly gent piped up, 'What is it for me?'

'Ask your trolley!' Ah, sweet retribution ...

Have you ever wondered what caddies talk about when we can't hear them? Things like, 'I've had some awful players in my time, but this feller ...'

Maybe they don't talk golf at all. They can certainly play the game, and they do give useful advice. More importantly, they can convince you they are right even when they are not.

Witness the irate golfer, who accuses, 'You said three iron – and it's short!' 'Ah yes,' says his caddie, 'but there's a lot of wind up there you can't see ...'

Or the golfer and caddie watching a sliced drive. 'Is that in trouble?' asks the former. 'Not yet, sir.'

In the game of golf, there are no surprises and all stories are true ... so they say.

Take the tale of the pro on the 18th hole, on the final day of the British Open. He is well down the fairway with his drive and only needs a par to win the championship.

'Five-iron, caddie.'

'Three.'

'Five-iron.'

'Three.'

'Are you sure?'

'Trust me ...'

The three-iron is hit, just as the wind comes up, pulling the ball down on to the green three inches from the hole. The pro taps in the easy putt and the championship is won.

'Thanks caddie,' he beams. 'But how did you know it was a three-iron?'

'I didn't,' the caddie confesses, 'but I'd already cleaned all the others.'

Do the pros suffer the same live-wire chat from their caddies as the amateurs? 'Of course,' said a pal of mine. Witness the legendary tale of the pro playing at Royal Dornoch, having just won the Open.

He asks his caddie, 'What's the line on this dog-leg?'

The caddie tells him, 'We play out to the right with a wee bit of draw, and the wind from the sea brings it back.'

'But I play with a fade,' says the pro.

Nevertheless the caddie insists, 'Play out to the right with a wee bit of draw, and the wind from the sea brings it back.'

The pro persists. 'But I play with a fade, I tell you, so I'll cut the corner off, shall I?'

'You do what you like,' says the caddie, 'but have you a spare ball in your bag?'

Subtle sarcasm, but well meant. And the story must be true – because it's about golf.

FIFTH HOLE

The Ladies, God Bless 'em

WHY CAN'T WE be more pragmatic? Why can't we be more realistic? Why can't we be more like the ladies, God bless 'em? Nobody – usually – has such a blissful outlook on golf.

'I keep topping the ball ... you know, catching the upper half,' the golfer says to his wife. 'Well, why don't you turn it over?' she advises.

'The motorised trolley won't go. The battery's flat,' he tells her. 'Oh dear, what shape should it be?' she asks.

And they are alive to all the excuses. 'Sorry I'm late, dear. I had a hole in one,' he says. 'Surely that meant you finished quicker,' she suggests. There's no answer to that.

In golf there should be a very special place for all the ladies – and I don't just mean on the forward tees. It is good to see clubhouses with whole families enjoying the fun. I look forward to mixed foursomes (who said 'gruesomes'?) – they are good for the game, part of the new face of golf.

But changes can be a long time coming in certain quarters. Who was it said: 'Golf means gentlemen only, ladies forbidden!' And who still believes it?

I heard a good story (and I have no reason to believe it's

Clubs to the tip

not true) from a snooty Home Counties club, where a party of ladies were sitting out on the verandah, watching a male four-ball coming up the 18th. One of the players obviously was heading for a very good score that only needed something like a par or a bogey to break the course record. But he duffed his second shot into the heather and it was totally unplayable. Understandably, he came out with a four-letter mouthful in sheer frustration.

On hearing this, one of the ladies got up and stormed into the secretary's office. 'This is disgusting,' she complained. 'I am out on the patio with a group of other ladies and we shouldn't have to put up with such disgraceful language from some of these so-called gentlemen – something should be done about it.'

The committee met and took it very seriously. After a long deliberation they decided the best way to prevent this embarrassment happening again was to ban ladies from the verandah ...

Playing at a well-known northern club, which, I might add, has its own ladies' course, and which you might think would be more liberal in its attitudes, Pat joined me as caddie and we had a very pleasant round. Coming off the 18th, my partner said, 'What's the round?'

'A pint, and a half of lager and lime, please,' I said.

'OK,' he said. 'See you in the bar. We'll pass Pat's out to her through the window.'

'What!!!!' Stand by for decibels from both of us.

'You see,' explained our flustered partner, 'I'm afraid the clubhouse is gents only. Ladies aren't allowed.'

'Well, you know what you and your club can do ...' and we both exited, our smiles now a mere grimace.

I got a fortnight of earache after that experience. 'I don't know why you bother with such a chauvinistic shower!'

'They're not all like that, dear. Honest!'

'Don't give me that. For two pins I feel like taking your clubs down the tip!'

'Don't do that love ... hey, you know that expensive dress you fancied last time we were in town ...' Thanks a lot, guys. Never again!

Pat is never backward in coming forward and making her feelings known. There was the time I played at Portmarnock just outside Dublin. That was the day I bought a brand new golf ball from the caddie, hit it off the first tee and it broke in two. I had to walk down both sides of the fairway to retrieve the pieces and take it back. Pat meanwhile was having problems of her own.

In the clubhouse she discovered she wasn't allowed to have a drink because she couldn't go into the main room – it was 'gentlemen only' again. So she complained bitterly to an important-looking chap who, when he could get a word in, said, 'I do agree, madam. I'm very sorry – but what can I do?'

When he walked away, one of his party came across to Pat and said, 'Do you know who that was?' and she replied, 'No.'

'That was the President,' she was told.

'The President of the golf club?' she asked. 'No,' he replied. 'The President of Ireland ...'

Ladies are capable of the most amazing feats on a golf course – and one I won't forget in a hurry occurred at Eastbourne, ideal for the 'in and out' golfer – a fine 18-hole course, and a short but equally good nine holes which can combine with 'the loop' to make a change whenever you feel like it. Here on the ninth hole of the short course, I saw my first hole in one. The distance was about 106 yards and a steady sand wedge on a still day was all that was really required.

Leaving the green one Saturday morning, I turned to see a wonderful combination on the tee. He was a slimmish chap, in his mid 60s, told to play golf for exercise to help a heart condition. She was of a similar age but portly and wearing a mackintosh (honest!), accompanying hubby for the sake of his health and her sanity, I guess.

She must have won the eighth because she stood first on the tee with (I later learnt) a two-wood (for 106 yards, remember!).

I saw the swing, the ball left the club at a height of two or three inches and bobbled gently but inexorably towards the green. Then as if by magic, it was drawn straight into the hole.

'Where did it go?' cried hubby, obviously myopic.

'In the hole,' I answered.

'Don't be damned ridiculous, man ...'

I moved away – never intervene between husband and wife, especially at times like these.

Later I saw the lady again in the pro shop, enquiring, 'I holed in one on the ninth. Do I get anything?'

'Yes – an eagle, luv,' replied the Scouse-born pro.

Truthfully, I have found that ladies love golf and I love the dignity they bring to it – steady swings, eagle-eyed putts, grace and, most importantly, competitive spirit.

I caddied once, and only once, for a lady in a club competition. We lost our drive on the fourth and spent ages searching heather and undergrowth while the opposition stood looking at her watch.

Eventually our opponent said, 'Your five minutes are up ... and by the way, your ball is over there!' Wow! Never again ...

On the other hand I had the great pleasure of playing a couple of holes with Mickey Walker, that lovely lady pro. It was at Foxhills in the Colonel Sanders Golf Classic.

Mickey was in great form – an elegant swing, no apparent effort. We played the first and waited on the second for the next team to come along – a trick I now use on corporate days. It makes for a long day but it is a great way to get to know the audience before the evening's speech.

It is a shame that we ask lady golfers to play on courses designed for men, and that to 'help' them we allow them to tee off nearer to the trouble.

I wonder if Mickey remembers the prize-giving at the Colonel Sanders Classic? I'll never forget it.

Having had one of those days when everything went right – I had recorded the longest drive, nearest the pin and best individual score – and not wishing to look too much of a 'smart alec' (remember Rudyard Kipling: 'Don't look too good, nor talk too wise') I offered a putter as a prize in the charity auction.

There had been a booby prize for the person who had lost the most balls and that had been 'won' by a man who claimed 22 balls adrift. Would you believe that this man bid for my putter! He'd never been near enough to a green to use one …

Mind you, that does pose an interesting question. Why reward the player who records the longest drive with a driver? Or the player who sinks the best putts with a putter? Seems there's a lot of 'Irish' logic to golf at times.

Prize-giving in golf to the amateur side always amuses me because they tend to give putters to the guy who has won. If he's won he's obviously putted very well, so what does he need a putter for? And they give drivers to the feller who has hit the longest drives. If he's hit the longest drive with the club he's got, why does he need another one?

On big golf days, the companies – Dunhills, Benson & Hedges – often give the celebrities and all partakers in the game a souvenir bag with Dunhill Masters on it or a golfing umbrella, or waterproofs and things, and these are as good a trophy as a celebrity would want because that's the kind of thing he's going to use as well as treasure.

You can tell how my golf has changed if you look in my

trophy cupboard. Because when I started off, if I appeared in anything or even won anything, I got a little tiny cup, a shield or a plaque. That has since gone on through the phase of the pewter mug to the crystal glass – which naturally I am always afraid to use – now I'm waiting for the day of the Teflon frying pan golf trophy.

Syd and Eddie of Little and Large, when they stage their Golf Classic, tend to come up with some novel prizes. A few years ago it was a little pair of bronze golf shoes on a plaque. That's what I call original.

Giving a winning celeb a bottle of champagne is not as satisfying as giving him a little certificate or plaque, or indeed something completely different. Gradually the world of golf is realising that it has got the right kind of prizes to hand out. It only takes a bit of thought.

SIXTH HOLE

The Courses – Beside the Seaside

I HOPE my shows have entertained seaside audiences as much as their golf courses have entertained me.

Come back with me to Gorleston Golf club, Great Yarmouth in the summer of 1977, with George Willard in charge of instruction and yours truly doing everything right – the right clubs, balls, a half decent swing and all day to practise and play. Here it was that I learned the value of the social side of golf – a good clubhouse and great members very tolerant of learners, particularly those who shout 'Fore' after every shot – just in case!

I remember my first par on the first – a three-wood, wedge and two putts. George told me on the green, 'Always remember the bucket principle. Get as near as the rim of a bucket and even you can't miss with the second putt ...' True enough, George, but the only putt I've ever been sure of was the fourth!

Gorleston's course runs along the seaside with the North Sea as a neighbour. Many is the time I've conceded defeat when cracking a drive over the edge and on to the beach below.

One of my favourite Gorleston stories features two of my heroes, not pro golfers but great amateur players and brilliant comedians. Arthur Askey and Ted Ray were

Cracking a drive over the edge and
on to the beach below

allegedly playing at Gorleston one afternoon. (I'm told for the Town Hall clock!). Here were two Scousers locked in mortal combat and Arthur was trying to slot in a two-foot putt. Out at sea were yachts gently tacking in the breeze when Arthur over-borrowed and totally missed this simple putt. Staring wilfully at Ted, he pointed out to sea and remarked, 'How can I putt with all that racket going on?'

Ted Ray also features in a story I heard about Torquay Golf Club. Torquay to me is almost like going home. Some of my best golf, happiest days and most traumatic moments are bound up in that club. I spent one long hot summer playing that lovely course and many enjoyable hours featuring in charity golf days with the members.

I learned never to have the honour when playing the sixth, because the climb is a real heart tester and you're better off losing the fifth in order to get your breath back.

Berni Flint, the much underrated singer and a golfer of very low handicap, had purloined an exploding ball from somewhere and while I was wheezing myself together again, switched it for mine on the tee.

Playing a three-iron for safety, I hit the ball straight and true, only to see a puff of blue smoke and the ball disintegrate about 150 yards away. I can't repeat my first expression (I think it was something like 'Golly heck!'). But my second was to ask for medical assistance.

'For you?' asked my partner.

'No,' I said. 'For Flint!'

But I digress. Ted Ray was playing a morning round at Torquay and striding down the superb 18th fairway following a good drive. To his left a mechanical digger was hard at work in the garden of a house, excavating a trench to lay drains. As he passed, Ted shouted to the digger driver: 'Don't bother on my account. It was only an old ball …'

*

After Yarmouth and my lessons and practice with patient George, Blackpool Opera House loomed, but top of the bill status prevented serious golf in 1978 – just the odd knock and hope that the swing stayed together for another time.

The Old Links, Royal Lytham, Fairhaven ... all lovely Lancashire courses and always a joy to play. Let me tell you, however, about Poulton-le-Fylde. I was staying out Poulton way in a sumptuous flat belonging to showbiz friends while entertaining the early holidaymakers at Blackpool's North Pier. The season included 2.30 p.m. matinées and thus prevented a full 18 holes. So we frequented Poulton-le-Fylde course, where a challenging nine holes was ideal for a comic seeking regular exercise.

The weather was good and the course so busy that it was imperative to book a starting time. So it was that I came across an amazing Scottish four-ball. They arrived fully clad for anything but golf – cut-away jeans, flip-flops, and no clubs.

Having been suitably equipped for the fray and provided with plenty of 'ammo', they enquired about the geography of the course. Obviously they were virtual beginners and the pro took kindly to them.

'Look,' he said, 'the chap in the green hat knows the course. He and his partner are off just before you. Follow them!'

Off went the Green Cap and his pal, followed rapidly but very erratically by the Scots, balls flying in all directions.

After about 40 minutes, the head Scot was back at the clubhouse. 'We need more balls, pal.'

'How's it going?' he was asked.

'Great.'

'Are you finding your way OK?'

'No problem. My pals are waiting on the fifth tee, and we've got the guy in the green hat there till I get back!'

Obviously they were taking no prisoners that day …

Staying with summer seasons, let me drift north-east to Bridlington, a great little town full of warm-hearted folk and good steady golfers, always willing to make up a game, no matter what.

Here at the Belvedere Road, a cliff-top course, prone to be windy, I met David Owen, a ten-handicapper, photographer and producer of the best hand-out pics I have ever had. He is my only witness to the reactions of British folk to the unexpected.

The local trams and buses were carrying a subtle advert for my summer show at the Spa Theatre – it involved a picture of me all of four feet tall.

The back nine holes at Bridlington pass the bus terminus at one point and on this summer morning David and I were teeing up, being watched by a dozen people on the upper deck of an open-topped bus. They looked at me, then over the side at the picture, then back to me again. And we could hear them arguing …

'Naw,' said the expert, 'it's not him. Too old and too poor. He's carrying his own clubs.'

As David took a practice swing, the expert exclaimed: 'God, he's missed it!'

We waited for the bus to pull away before drawing breath – and collapsing in a heap!

Golf was fun at Bridlington, and the fun began even before the season opened. I always arrive a couple of days early for a season or a panto, to 'bed in', sort out digs and parking, and make for the golf course – though not necessarily in that order.

I contacted the theatre on the Friday to see if anyone was available for a round of golf on Saturday morning and was put in touch with the captain of Flamborough Head Golf Club, who in turn put me on to the proprietor of a local hotel.

Mike was a two-handicapper, a great bloke and heavily overworked in the catering trade. But he was delighted to oblige, and we agreed to meet at about 8.15 on the Saturday morning.

He was full of smiles when he arrived and after two or three holes of getting to know each other, he spilled the beans on the 'joke of the day'.

The night before, Mike had said to his wife, 'Give me a shout at seven in the morning, luv.'

She said, 'You never get up early on a Saturday. What's up tomorrow?'

'I'm playing a quick round of golf, that's all.'

'Oh yes, and who's free to spend three hours playing golf with you at peak booking time?'

'It's Tom O'Connor, luv!'

The good lady said nothing for a few minutes and then announced, 'When you come home, Mike, I may not be here. I'm going shopping.'

'Who are you going to the shops with, luv?'

'Barbra Streisand!' came the snappy reply.

We played Flamborough Head, a tricky course made even trickier by the fact that most of the morning it was covered in mist.

'The line is roughly there …'

'Can you see the lighthouse? Well, it's that way … about an eight-iron.'

'I've pulled that drive – where would you say it was?'

'Gone!'

We stopped for tea at a small café halfway round the course. I still can't believe that the folk in that little village still left their doors unlocked. Was it ever like that where I lived?

Maybe this wasn't Flamborough after all. Maybe it was Brigadoon, and Mike was really Gene Kelly … No, with that beautiful swing, he had to be for real!

*

Along the coast to Scarborough. The year is 1981 and I am playing the South Cliff golf course. Next to my home course, I have probably played this one more often than any other, so often, in fact, that I indulge in a mental round of golf at South Cliff if I can't get to sleep! It's much more interesting than counting sheep, or whatever … I wonder if other golfers do the same! My best score on the first is a three – a three-wood, a nine-iron and one putt. On the second, another birdie … It's amazing how you can break 60 by remembering only the good holes!

Denis Taylor was the pro at South Cliff in my day – a good teacher, Yorkshire born and proud of the fact that he'd never been out of the county!

'We're standing tall and we're remembering tempo,' he would stress. It was great to play a round with a man who could almost anticipate your next mistake.

He once admitted to me that when he first arrived at the club, he'd played a practice round and shanked three consecutive shots. 'I don't think I'm going to like it here!' he told the secretary. But thankfully he stayed. He was a good man and those were good days.

They were also days of practicing with Alberto, a Spaniard, a collector of drivers and any gadget that would lengthen his drive.

'This driver hits the ball ten further yards,' he would enthuse; or 'This Pinnacle ball goes ten further yards.' Many a day I would see him with a bucket full of balls and half a dozen weird and wonderful woods lined up ready to be 'auditioned'.

'He's got all those drivers – he only needs a conductor,' I heard one wag say.

Alberto, in fact, was leader of a Latin singing group called Los Zafiros, a great support act, professional and very entertaining.

He was also the owner of the longest back swing I have ever seen. Only the ground or his left ankle prevented it going full circle. It was amazing to watch him play a weeny sand shot with the same action as his drive!

Here was a man who claimed he once won 60 (or was it 600) balls from Jimmy Tarbuck on the putting green. The story goes that Alberto turned up at a particular golf club looking for a game and found Tarby on the putting green. 'Fancy a quick nine holes?' he suggested. 'Play you for a ball a hole ...' And, of course, Alberto won. 'OK,' said Tarby. 'Double or quits' – probably not realising that double or quits can apply to each hole. It's amazing how it all adds up. Actually I've always been too scared to question Tarby about this tale ...

Anyway, here at South Cliff, with Alberto, Denis and many other partners, I played some of the best golf of my life. How? Put it down to early nights, a two-mile jog in the morning to loosen up, 50 practice balls, ten minutes' putting practice and then off to the first tee. But why does it feel like cheating?

Probably because real golfers jump out of the car, change shoes in the car park with one foot on the bumper, then scurry to the tee, take a single practice swipe and lurch into the ball. Then, if their shoulder is still in its socket, they clump off round the course, attempting to shake off last night's hangover and lack of sleep.

It is possible to play 18 holes in that condition – and actually forget some of the holes you've played. How many times have you had to consult your card to see what happened back on the fourth? 'Did I really par that hole ... surely I would have remembered!'

But golf is all about remembering, isn't it? At rabbit level we remember only the good shots. At ten-handicap and below we only remember the bad ones ... 'Did I really pull that five iron into a gale?' 'How? ... Why? ... What am I doing!'

And you are ready to blame everyone except yourself. 'What a brainless twit I was to let this guy talk himself

into caddying for me! I asked for a six-iron, he gave me a nine and without checking I hit it. Now the gallery are playing a new game show – Spot the Prat!'

Incidentally, Scarborough was where I first heard of the Henry Cotton ploy of swinging a club against an old car tyre to strengthen the wrists. It works for sure, and I gained the nickname of 'Wristy O'Connor' for a long time, although the actual cause of my 'wristitis' was human, not inanimate.

At South Cliff club there was a young boy, maybe 17, who hung around the pro-shop practising day and night. It seemed he always had time to play a round and he hit the longest iron shot I'd ever seen.

His entire set-up was wrong (well, not 'wrong' really, just not orthodox. After all, what's 'right' in golf?) He kept his legs nearly together, his stance was high and gangly, his swing went nowhere – just up and down in a narrow wristy arc – but when he connected with an eight-iron it flew as far as my five.

All right – so he probably closed the face of the club, and I could have hit my five-iron better – but not much!

Purist members of the club would say: 'It's all very well, but it's all to do with split-second timing. He's got no margin of error. When his timing goes on a bad day he'll be all over the place.'

I was there 14 weeks and this lad never had a bad day. I even tried to copy his style because it was effortless, all wrist and no shoulder. I had many bad days – roughly seven a week.

But the lad gave me a little light relief during this period, except for the 'straw ball' incident.

I was playing down a long par four, hit a goodish drive and was looking for a five-wood to make the green. Unlike most of my efforts at that time, the five-wood flew 'straight out of the screws' (I think that's the expression) like a bullet, connecting just before its zenith with a baling machine crossing the fairway. The ball was baled in straw and never seen again – and no one could give me a ruling for laughing!

On my last day at the club I was presented with a bale of straw containing a golf ball – a Commando Cross-out as I recall. Very funny, lads!

SEVENTH HOLE

Hospitality and Hostilities

GANTON is a super course which would test the very best. It's the only place where I've seen a window cleaner's ladder in a bunker – boy, it's a deep one!

During my Scarborough summer season, I was lucky enough to get a game at Ganton, thanks to a kind fan who was also a member.

I was slotted into a four-ball with three of the 'youth club' – all over 75 and still steady golfers, but prevented from making a full shoulder turn by the attentions of Father Time. Direction and control had superseded length in their game, but at least it kept them together on the fairway.

My self-appointed coach was a lovely man called Cecil, who I swear was still using the first ball he ever hit. He never missed a fairway, and never missed a green – albeit not in regulation – but he wasn't up to advising a young upstart comic who was knocking 'em long.

'What club is it here, Cecil?' I would ask.

'Four-iron,' he'd say confidently, and – whoosh! – I'd find myself clearing the green and landing in deadly serious undergrowth, Apache country as they say.

'I can't understand it. That's what I use!' Cecil would wail.

'In future,' I suggested, 'just give me the approximate yardage'; but it still did no good. I remember being in no fewer than 12 bunkers in 18 holes – must be some kind of record!

At least I finished on a par, which always looks good in front of the clubhouse. The knack is trying to look disappointed at only parring the hole. It's good for the ego – as long as no one asks to see your score card!

I really must play Ganton again one of these days. I hope the 'youth club' is still there. I'm sure they must be ... good guys like that live forever, don't they?

On to The Belfry, and many more happy memories, not just of the golf but of the wonderful hotel facilities and the many conferences I have addressed. It is a great set-up there, complemented by smashing staff!

I will always remember the courses at The Belfry for the tragi-comic circumstances surrounding my performances. I remember the long par four dog-leg over the water, for instance. You may know the one I mean – it's where Sevvy once drove the green.

Did I drive it too? Did I heck! Under John Jacobs's instruction I played safe. It was the final day of the BMW Classic, always a day to remember. John and I were playing with the UK boss of BMW – and for money, as I recall.

'Do yourself a favour,' said John. 'Take a five-iron down the left, and then a nice little chip to the flag over the water.' Sure as eggs, I hit a blinding five-iron to the perfect spot. There was appreciative applause from the gallery accompanied by that heart-warming opinion from the great man: 'If you could have walked down and placed the ball, you couldn't have put it in a better spot. That's perfect!'

So down the fairway I strode, the epitome of Mr Cool, and took a quick look into the distance at the flag, before hatching my next plan. I reckoned it was a sand wedge, high in the air: plonk the ball by the stick and hope it grabs tight on the green and stays.

Action! I took a gentle swing with the sand wedge, and up went the ball. I lobbed it straight into the water! What was it the gods of golf once decreed: 'There is absolutely nothing more embarrassing in the whole world than a duffed chip!'

Sorry John – your plan was perfect, but your pupil wasn't up to the job.

Let's fast forward to the Brabazon course on another day, and another corporate function. This time I am playing in a four-ball, and there is no particular problem, except that it is foggy, very foggy. A shotgun start, and we're off the 12th, or any hole we can actually find.

We tee off and follow the vague direction of our drives. Amazingly we find them all and most of our second shots too. Gradually it becomes easier, we think, to play in this grey shroud ... or is it?

Suddenly, to coin a phrase, the wheel comes off the bike and we find ourselves scrambling round a dog-leg of uncertain length – and meeting another four-ball doing exactly the same, but coming the other way!

'Are you with our Society?' we call.

'No – we're with the Woolwich!' comes the jovial reply, a humorous topicality in those days but of absolutely no help to us, cast adrift and possibly lost forever.

Obviously we didn't die of exposure, though it was a close run thing. Eventually we contacted friendly life and returned to the right track, several balls shorter and much wiser. In future, I decide, there is a simple weather rule – if helicopters don't fly what chance have golfers got?

The pros have to be part diplomat, part wise-guy, with the right answers for any number of awkward occasions. When I played at Moore Park, a super course, in the Coca

Cola Classic, my caddie, a charming fellow called John who used to be caddie-master but has now retired and just comes out for celebrity events, gave us the lovely story about the lady who went up to the golf pro and said, 'I want a ruling and I want it now!' So the pro asked, 'What's the probem?' She said, 'I want to know what's the penalty for playing an air shot over somebody else's ball ...' Now as far as I can see that penalty should be three – one for playing the air shot and two for someone else's ball. But the pro's problem is to determine whether she's asking on behalf of herself or her opponent. It's one of those occasions where you have to think twice before you answer.

It was a golf pro, I might add, who in my very early days shamed me into appearing in a charity tournament, the George Elrick Classic at Royal Eastbourne. George, the perennial Housewives' Choice, is a lovely man, much talented and devoted to charitable works. Furthermore, he was just the spark I needed to get into golf for fund raising.

He had organised a great day complete with teams, sponsors, starter, media coverage, everything you could wish for – and more, as it turned out. For there were also watering holes at the ninth and 18th, and they were to be the source of my woes on this day.

Not being up to the standard of the bulk of players I chose to go off last with another 'rabbit' – but this guy had been practising! After eight I was eight down, the sort of situation that merited two more holes and an early bath, I thought. But no – he contrived to lose his ball on the ninth and somehow I scrambled a half in eight!

So we came to the café at the ninth – and what a difference a stop makes.

'I don't drink, but you have a jar,' insists the rabbit.

'I'm not fussy,' says I.

'Go on, do you good ...' he urges.

'Really I'd rather play on,' I say truthfully.

'Look,' he persists. 'You have a quickie and I'll join you.'

'Oh all right. I'll have a can of lager please,' I say resignedly.

'In that case I'll have a wee treble Scotch,' says the rabbit.

Several wee trebles later I find myself assisting my 'oppo' to the tenth tee and winding him round a ball washer while I tee off, he having hit his drive 200 yards straight up, his ball dropping almost between his feet.

I coasted easily round to the 18th and a one-hole victory, only encumbered by having to drag a blathering partner from rough to rough in search of his ball.

Mentally I felt elated at my amazing comeback, physically I felt as if I'd gone 15 rounds with Muhammad Ali, and morally I was disturbed to discover I had helped pander to the cravings of a reformed alcoholic – whose wife still hasn't forgiven me ...

A victory is still a victory, but so is a defeat, and I'll always remember Eastbourne for my most unusual one. George Elrick, by the way, did it to me. I was playing a few holes with him, feeling great and on the green in two, while he had duffed his second shot deep into the foliage and was snarling and calling on the Lord.

Suddenly, his shot fired out of the undergrowth and, following two ricochets off trees, I realised his seven-iron had somehow guided his ball 140 yards or more – out of trouble, over sand, two bounces and into the hole for a birdie. What a fluke!

He had no idea what he had done, of course, but the shot so unnerved me, I three-putted and took a five. Three holes later he was taking a fiver off me as coolly as if he knew what he'd been doing all the time. Watch the Scots – they are dangerous foes!

I have known good days, bad days, and special days. Days when you do something so amazing you desperately yearn for witnesses who will talk, or even live coverage on News at Ten.

I had such a moment while summer seasoning on the Isle of Wight, a quite incredible place, ideal for relaxing. In addition to beautiful scenery and genial residents, plus the best in yachting and boating, it has a self-imposed 14 mph speed limit, as the roads are dominated by tractors, caravans and most other vehicles that just can't be passed. It's a good thing that the Isle of Wight encourages dawdlers otherwise it would be a very frustrating place indeed.

It is, in any event, perfect territory for a memorable summer season – I can't recall opening as many garden fêtes before or since, but that's all part of the fun.

Sandown golf club is the venue for this tale. It is a summer's morning and there is time to play only the front nine, on my own …

The shot of the year, fortunately, comes on the first and is witnessed by two roofers atop the clubhouse.

'We seen your oppo here last year, you know,' they tell me.

'Who?'

'Jimmy Tarbuck. He played great.'

'You ain't seen nothin' yet,' says I.

I have two chances now – either hit a good 'un and become a name worth quoting, or a duff one and hope they think it was a gag to impress them. I stand up to the ball, take three practice swings and – bang! I connect with one that almost reaches the green, a good 260 yards, starts low and climbs. You know the one – it looks like it's still climbing even as it stops. It has a nice bit of draw on it and is ideally positioned for the second shot.

'Wow,' comes the gasp from the roof.

I tell myself, 'Keep calm … try to look disappointed!' I say casually, aloud and to no one in particular, 'Too far. I really wanted a full wedge for my second. Must use an iron next time.'

'BLIMEY HE'S BACK IN
THE BUNKER AGAIN!'
SANDOWN
GOLF CLUB

'D'you hear that?' says the roof. 'He's not happy. What a player …'

Wait until you play there again, Tarby. I can just hear them … 'That grey-haired mate of yours! What a guy – knocks 'em out of sight!'

I just hope they aren't still watching as my second goes into the bunker greenside, or when my third and fourth are also played from the same bunker.

EIGHTH HOLE

Scotland and Ireland

LET'S MOVE north of the border to bonnie Scotland – lovely scenery, exquisite courses, the home of golf and many a good player.

Those Scottish golf courses are really something else. Ray Floyd was in a light aircraft flying over the Firth of Forth one time and he asked a fellow passenger, 'What's that below?'

'That's the Forth,' he was told.

Ray thought for a moment, then said, 'Hell of a carry ...'

Two consecutive winters I did pantomime in Inverness, and it gave me the chance to play at Nairn and Inverness golf clubs. In all those winter weeks, both years, I only failed to play on one day, and that because snow lay on the greens. I even played on New Year's Day, despite the head that needed calming with many paracetamols and the stomach churning in the way that only whisky can make it churn. It was here I learned that Hogmanay means 'Help me up!'

I often long for the pleasures of northern Scotland and never miss a chance to visit. So it was that I came across the Boat of Garten club. Together with a pal, Jim, and his good lady, my wife Pat and I spent a week based in

Inverness, touring the area playing golf.

We found Boat of Garten on a day when no one else was there. The clubhouse was empty, and there were no players in sight. There was just a note explaining the procedure – place the fee in an envelope, write your car number on the envelope and place it in the honesty box. Amazing!

It was an interesting day's golf. For a start, Jim lost his temper – I had never seen this before. He lay on the grass beside the ball screaming, 'Will you go into the hole!!' It didn't work – he three-putted.

So much for Mike Burton's belief that in every ball there is a little pilot steering it in and out of mischief. Why else does a ball do things for which there is no rational explanation? This uncertainty probably explains why it is more of an achievement to stop a ball inches away from the pin on a par three rather than hole in one – which, as we have established, is a fluke shot anyway!

In Scotland I was questioned about my handicap. 'Ten,' I answered truthfully.

'Which course?' they demanded. So you can't talk a good game up there. You are judged, quite rightly, on ability and performance.

My solitary foray into entertaining the Scots was equally traumatic – not only on Hogmanay but also live on television!

In the early 1980s I was chosen to host *The Hogmanay Show* live from the beautiful Gleneagles Hotel. It may sound like a fairy tale, but it just about ended in nightmare for me!

We had a great cast: Moira Anderson, Maggie Moone, the late great Chic Murray, plus more singers, bands, raconteurs, a live and lively audience. It just couldn't go wrong – could it?

The rehearsals went OK, but I wasn't that happy about

the sound level. To me it seemed too quiet for a room full of Hogmanay revellers. In retrospect, a lot of things were assumed to be in order, when today they would have been checked and rechecked. Items already recorded on video tape were intended as back-up – the 'belt and braces' approach, as they say, in case of emergency – and boy, did we need them!

The show opened with the Britannia Airways Pipe Band outdoors, playing us in through the main doors and into the dining room, full of guests in great spirits.

After a song from Moira and a bit of opening chat, I already realised that the audience noise was louder than the sound system. But still we pressed on with various items, including some recorded material.

Then the pipe band came back. They sounded wounderful, but at the end of their piece, things began to go seriously awry. The mark for poor old Chic was covered by furniture which had been moved while the audience settled down, and consequently cameras were not at the correct angle to pick up the right shots, links started to go adrift and we began to race headlong into a mini-shambles.

I couldn't wait for the end of the show, but even then there was no relief. Sitting quietly with Pat, Maggie Moone and her husband, we found ourselves analysing our futures following this débâcle.

Hopefully, we convinced ourselves, nobody would have been watching: they would all have been out celebrating themselves. At least nobody important in the world of television would have been watching it … would they? Eventually I admitted that Maggie might salvage some pride from the show, but I reckoned I was doomed. There was only one thing for it – a round of early morning golf to lift the blues.

Somehow, at eight in the morning, despite much quaffing of the 'falling down liquid', I staggered out to play a very important 18 holes. For some reason, my head was in perfect shape for the game. I couldn't have cared less, I felt all was lost and I really wasn't bothered. If you could bottle that feeling, I reckon we'd all have a chance of winning the US Masters …

I clocked up a par, par, birdie, birdie, par, birdie. Maybe it was me keeping my head extra still – only because even the slightest excess movement sent it spinning. Or perhaps it was my slow deliberation over every shot – simply to prevent me falling asleep.

Up to the ninth it was the best round of golf I had ever played, but then human failure began to creep in. Suddenly the devil began: 'If you can protect this score you could be well under par at the finish.' Ah yes, when that little voice starts nagging at your brain, it's the kiss of death. That's when I took an iron off the tee for safety, topped the drive, duffed the second, three-putted on the green. Down for six – aargh!

Anyway, I still finished with a very good personal score and returned to the hotel delighted and relieved to learn I was not being made a scapegoat for the previous evening's disaster. All in all, it was quite a weight off my shoulders!

But the formula for a great nine holes remains my legacy of that fateful Hogmanay. It is easy to set up: merely do something so chaotic that it puts your whole future, your entire career in jeopardy, then soften up the brain with the juice of the glen, assume all is lost – and relax! Even so, I wouldn't recommend it as a regular tonic.

I have played courses north and south of the border in Ireland, too, and find them just as relaxing in their own way.

I will never forget one time at Royal Portrush on a day that the heavens forgot. In seven holes we suffered hell, high water, hurricane and rain like bullets on the skin. Soon it was too cold to grip the bag, never mind the clubs, so we decided to creak back to the clubhouse.

As we stood there, wrapping our purple frames around large warming brandies, we watched a video of Sevvy doing endless tricks with a putter.

I said to my blue-nosed Irish partner, 'Isn't he just wonderful?'

Ken sniffed, and said, 'Ah yes – but can he tile a roof?'

Seemed, really, to put the day into some kind of perspective!

NINTH HOLE

Up in the World

BEAUTIFUL WOBURN is a regular date on my calendar, marking my yearly trip to play in the Dunhill Masters pro-celebrity tournament. To think that a kid from the back streets of Bootle could ever be invited to play each year on this stately course and join the likes of Berhard Gallagher, Sevvy, Ronan Rafferty – sometimes I just know I am a very lucky man.

The set-up is a Texas scramble with pros, celebrities and two or three amateurs connected with Dunhill or its sales groups. A Texas Scramble is one of those combinations designed to speed up the game on the day. In a four-ball, the team takes the best drive and each player hits his second shot from that spot. Then the third shot is taken from where the best second lands. And so on. Theoretically you should be in with a birdie chance at each hole.

It is akin to playing a greensome, where each pair picks the better of their drives, then the partner plays the second shot, and so on in turn.

The best greensome story I heard involved Tony Jacklin playing with a little old lady. They teed off and took his drive. She hit the ball into the bushes, and he went across and hacked it out in line with the green. She slammed the ball into a bunker on the edge of the green. He chipped out of the bunker and luckily it went straight into the hole. So he said to her, 'Now look luv, we'll have to steady up. This is a par four and we took a five then,' to which she replied, 'Yes – but you played three of 'em.'

In Liverpool, instead of a greensome we play a yellowsome, where instead of you and your partner electing the better shot, the opposition has the choice. The legendary yellowsome story is of two guys: one who holed in one and the other who put his ball in the bushes. The opposition chose the ball in the bushes as the better shot – so the hole in one didn't count!

Anyway, back to Woburn, here it was, in my first year, that I met an unforgettable character – Peter Barnes.

Big Peter is the most genial of men with a great sense of humour, brilliant wit and a perfect laugh for a struggling comic. Here is a man who eschews the niceties of the club maker – woods, long irons, short irons, and the rest. Peter hits everything with a five-iron. 'It saves a lot of messing,' he explains. I suppose he's right.

It was Peter who, coming back to England after a tournament abroad, bemused Customs officials who suspected him of bringing in a new full set of clubs, by showing them 'the trusty five' worn to a wafer with constant use.

But my all-time favourite memory of this great fellow, great friend and amazing sponsor of charity tournaments, was watching him actually playing the 18th at Woburn – and missing an 18 in putt.

Said the pro, who shall be nameless, 'My nine-year-old daughter would have holed that one!'

'Oh really,' remarked Peter, 'and how many cigarettes does she sell?'

Still at Woburn, and in another year of the Dunhill Masters, I was in the team with Ronan Rafferty, a nice guy and a very good golfer. I hit a screamer on the first and as it was Texas Scramble, I raced down the fairway to show the gallery that we were going to use my ball. Four chips (one each) and one putt and we were down in three – a birdie is always a good start.

Feeling really good, we moved to the second tee and as we prepared to tee off we heard the crowd behind us screaming approval as Sevvy chipped in for an eagle! Nothing else for it but to bite your lip and keep saying, 'But can he tile a roof?' Bah!

Moving house from Birkdale to Ascot was obviously time to break new ground. Although I had lived many years in the Southport area, it wasn't until I left that I really got into the golf swim up there. But the serious stuff began as I got used to my new home club, Royal Ascot. I guess I imagined it to be one of those clubs where you have to wear a collar and tie in the showers, but truthfully I have been very happy there and made quite a few down-to-earth friends.

I prepared myself with daily visits to local driving ranges and steady practice with a bag of balls and an upturned umbrella on the lawn before I ventured out for my first 18 holes.

Situated in the centre of Royal Ascot race course, the golf course has all a golfer can desire – heather, a water hazard, a cricket pitch, public rights of way all over the place – an ideal course to play a visitor for money!

I was introduced to the course by Dick Richardson, former European heavyweight boxing champion and one of the hardest hitters of the ball I've seen – with no backswing!

Here I also met John O'Neill, then captain and for many years club chairman, a Dublin man who in those days never used any club larger than a four-iron. I believe he's matured now!

John has been a great friend and partner to me, so

He has a putter like Harry Lauder's walking stick

much so that he probably won't mind me saying that his is without doubt the worst swing in golf history. If Moses had seen his swing, there'd have been another commandment.

He also has a putter like Harry Lauder's walking stick … but he is in truth a great partner. Overall I think we've only lost once while playing together, and there's a secret to this.

I 'lamp' one a long way, hopefully, then John lays up with a four-iron, swung like no other. This has two effects: the opposition can't believe the swing contortions, and his effort makes mine look twice as long and demoralises the others.

We played together on the day that Royal Ascot launched its new par five hole (now the first, then the third) and the gods were kind to me.

Following a three-wood and a five-wood, I holed a 12 ft putt for a three. Needless to say it was all I did all day, but I couldn't wait to tell the clubhouse.

I entered all smiles and announced, 'I've just eagled the par five.'

'So have I,' said old Bill, sat in the corner. Bill is a grand old character, 80 plus, so I ask him, 'What did you use?'

'Three three-woods.'

I've often mused how long it took him to realise his third shot was in the hole.

Bill was the first person I saw use an eleven-wood. In fact he had a bag full of woods, down to a thirteen I think. It looked like Sherwood Forest in there.

He was a steady player, always down the middle, landing just short of the green, always putting for par, but he was no help to a stranger, club-wise.

'What is it for me, Bill?'

'I don't know, but I use an eleven-wood with half a swing.'

Try converting that to an iron …

While we are rambling around Royal Ascot, let me tell

you about my 'almost hole in one'. Some years ago, the second hole (now the seventh) was a short par three, and John O'Neill and I teed up on a bright summer's afternoon.

John hit an eight-iron and his ball landed 3 feet away from the pin, which brought a satisfied smile to his lips.

I also took an eight-iron and hit the ball beautifully, even if I say so myself. It flew right to the flag, striking it, and fell stone dead an inch from the rim of the hole.

As we both strode towards the green muttering something about, 'If Peter Alliss could see those shots he'd want to play a round with us!' we were approached by a charming lady clad in a mini-dress and sporting and advertising sash. She called out, 'Congratulations. You've won! You're the nearest!'

'Say nothing …' said John, preparing to walk on.

Apparently the Society before us had been sponsored by a well-known drinks company based in 'Varrington', and the 'nearest the pin' prize for the day was a giant bottle of vodka. Protesting (but ever so slightly), we accepted the prize and finished the round, subsequently joining the Society in the clubhouse and explaining everything. They pressed us to keep the prize, even though we weren't officially with their party (which, of course, we did, although secretly trading it for the equivalent in Scotch with the club steward!)

From my home these days I'm only a short distance from many great clubs – Sunningdale, Wentworth and so on. There is plenty of scope for golfing enjoyment and for meeting interesting people.

Take Paul, a long-time member of Wentworth, a good player and a gentleman, always polite and a marvellous teller of tales.

I'll never forget a 'friendly' we played when, after 13 holes, he'd kindly allowed me to be all square, such was his prowess. We were standing on the 14th tee of the west course facing 160 yards, all uphill – not an easy prospect.

Paul pointed out the green-keeper's hut on the right of the fairway and asked if I had heard the sad story about it. I fell for it and said, 'No, please tell me …'

Apparently, Paul went on, nine years before, in a Sunday morning mixed foursome, a man had teed off, duffed his shot and his ball had landed behind the shed.

'Play it out sideways to the fairway,' he told his wife, 'and I'll try to chip us somewhere near the flag.'

But she had other ideas. 'There's a door at this end,' she said. 'If there's one at the other end, open it and I'll try to play through …'

For some reason he complied, opened the far door and watched her strike an iron straight at the door frame. The richochet hit her between the eyes and killed her outright. Her husband understandably never played again.

Eight years later, however, he was persuaded to go out on another Sunday morning round, 'just to give it a try,' and by a billion to one chance his ball performed exactly the same feat on the 14th and landed behind the self-same shed again.

'Shall I try to play it through if you hold the door open?' enquired his new lady partner.

'Get lost!' he replied. 'Last time I took a seven …'

Good story, Paul – it had me fooled right up to the tag-line!

Wentworth is a fine club with fine courses and brings back many happy memories.

The first trophy I ever won, the Panasonic Pro-Celebrity-Am, partnering Bernard Hunt, another gentleman and a great player, was won with no help from me.

Among the many celebrities that day was the legendary

wartime hero Douglas Bader, sadly no longer with us. I recall he played very well that day, his team losing to us by the odd point.

My lasting memory of that day is of a young cub reporter covering the game and asking Douglas why he used a shooting stick when walking the course. Was it perhaps to keep his balance?

'No,' smiled the great man. 'It's to stop these legs running away from me on the slopes!' God bless him – he was a fierce competitor and it was a privilege to meet him.

Of the Wentworth courses, I guess the east course is my favourite; not so long as the Burma Road, but just as interesting and, I think, just as difficult.

Whenever I had time at home in the summer I would join Mike Burton, possibly Russ Abbot and Shakin' Stevens for a knock. It is a great way to relax with fellow artistes; plenty of gags, but no quarter asked or given.

However, in all my golfing days and in all the elite company I have enjoyed, the most remarkable and incredible incident happened to me at Wentworth.

It was a Saturday morning, members and guests only, first up, first served, with golf balls in the chute to determine pecking order. I'd been signed in by my ex-manager and had put in a monogrammed ball as our place in the queue.

When our turn came, I eagerly took my 'Won from Tom O'Connor' ball from the chute and proceeded to tee up.

A man raced to the tee and shouted, 'It's our turn!' I pointed out that he had no ball in the chute and replied, 'I did have – it's down the fairway now!'

Apparently, several four-balls ago, he had played his drive down the first, then sat waiting for his partner to finish getting ready in the clubhouse. No thought that, as a member, he should have known the rule that all players in his party must be present before teeing off. No thought that many another player could have picked up his drive as a 'find'.

I prayed – as you would – that his ball was gone, but it was still there. Drat! It ruined my day!

TENTH HOLE

Golf, TV and Me

PROBABLY THE hardest thing to do in life is to make an extremely intricate task look easy. It's an art bestowed on very few people.

In soccer, Beckenbauer had the art, as did Pele and Gordon Banks.

In horse racing, Arkle, Red Rum, Millhouse were really special. In boxing, Sugar Ray Robinson and Muhammad Ali had the gift.

We can each compile our own special list of accomplished sporting folk, those who have given us pleasure simply watching what they do and watching them do it well.

In other fields of endeavour, too, we can find and appreciate people who make what they do seem so simple. Witness the ease with which Bruce Forsyth hosts a television show – such professionalism, such dynamism, and yet apparently something you or I reckon we could do just as well because it looks so effortless.

Forget it! I've tried it and I have to tell you it is not as easy as it looks. For behind Bruce's easy-going smile, the funny banter and the seeming nonchalance there is a whole lifetime of experience, hard work, highs and lows – and most important of all, a special gift.

Nothing to it!

So it is with golf, our favourite sport (I guess that's right, otherwise I wouldn't be writing and you wouldn't be reading!) Golf looks deceptively simple when watched from a warm armchair with beer in one hand and the TV remote control in the other. A drive, a five-iron, two putts maximum ... nothing to it. On to the next tee ... easy game. No wind, no pressure, no problem ... anyone can do it. Makes you feel it's hardly worth trying it for yourself. Better to find something tricky to play – like darts.

Television may have made sports such as snooker and golf more popular but it has also given people a false idea that they are easy to play. They see Steve Davis or Sevvy doing something fantastic and then hope to emulate them on the table or on the course the next day. Remember when you used to go for a suit to Burtons? If it needed altering they would do it while you waited and to pass the time, you could go upstairs and have a game of snooker – at least you could in Liverpool!

And if you think of it in terms of our very first games of snooker, remember breaking off, splitting the pack and scattering the reds everywhere? Your mate would say, 'You twit!' Yet if Steve Davis plays the same shot on television, the commentator whispers things like, 'There's an awful lot of pressure on the game here at the Crucible. There has to be a reason for that bold move ...' So it's all a matter of values.

Golf is a game of opposites really. You and I can do things that make others exclaim, 'You twit – what have you done that for!' Whereas if Trevino does it there is obviously a deep hidden meaning. But the one thing we must not do is say to ourselves, 'If it's good enough for Trevino, it's good enough for me!' As soon as you do that, you start on the path to a round of 95.

Moreover, golf, like snooker, gives a totally wrong impression when viewed on the small box. There is no hint of the agonising hours of practice required; the soul searching, the bottling of emotions as a player stands over a putt. It may be only 2 feet, but it could also be the difference between abject failure and glorious immortality.

If one man could be said to have changed the way we see the game of golf, it must be Severiano Ballesteros.

You may agree with me that the future of TV coverage of golf, and the subsequent popularity of the game for spectator and player, was boosted enormously by the sight of a young Ballesteros in the British Open.

Here was a kid defying everything the text-books said should be done and playing as none of the 'correct' players had done before. He never played safe, he seemed hardly ever to be on the fairway, even playing one shot from the car park. You could hear the armchair critics saying to themselves, 'What is going on? Maybe this game isn't so easy after all. Maybe I'll go and try for myself ... see if I can play straight all the time. Maybe I'll go and watch real-life golfers on the courses and get the proper feel of the game.'

Sevvy became everyman's hero, and TV became a major part of golf lore. By satellite we can now watch our favourite players all over the world. Videos help us learn from the greats. Videos of our own game can help us iron out faults.

Television is here to stay, and truthfully it can enable us to see the funny side sometimes too.

My daughter Anne Marie lives in Italy, married to a charming Italian who thinks Nigel Mansell is the second coming – poor chap, he knows only cars.

Some years ago Christy O'Connor Jnr was leading the Open overnight, and leading well. Anne's husband Rocco was watching it on satellite TV and all he saw was Christy's back view, grey hair peeking from beneath his cap, and the name O'Connor.

'Hey,' he called to Anne, 'your father's leading the British Open.'

Before she could take stock of this astounding feat, Christy turned round and Rocco added, 'Oh no, it's not your dad – this chap is far too young and good looking.' One to you, Christy!

I must admit my own TV golfing debut (the pro-celebrity event I already mentioned in passing) was fraught with trepidation. Hosted by Peter Alliss, I found myself partnering Sandy Lyle, and playing against two legends, Lee Trevino in golf and one of my showbiz heroes, Jimmy Tarbuck.

You have got to remember that although I'd worked many thousands of hours on TV, it did not include any type of sport. In fact it only covered my job as a comic and quiz show host. Like everyone else, I am confident and cool doing the things I'm trained for, but suddenly to have my hobby, and my shortcomings, scrutinised at very short range was a nightmare.

Funnily enough, I wasn't too bothered about the cameras. 'They'll cut out the worst bits,' I thought. It was the gallery that frightened me.

But the gods were on my side. They gave us weather like only Turnberry can enjoy, a freezing, biting wind and torrential rain! Consequently there was no gallery – thank you, Lord!

We had a quick warm-up on the practice ground during which Trevino dropped a ball into sloppy earth and hit it with a one-iron more than 250 yards. It hardly left the ground all the way. 'Wind shot,' he explained. I thought to myself, 'It's no use making a note of that. I'll never be able to play it!'

On the first tee, Tarby attempted to keep us smiling, a herculean task in this weather even for the 'guv'nor'.

The cameras were set and ready to roll, and Trevino was over his ball. 'You know, Tommy,' he said to me, 'Americans never play a practice shot in the wet.' The next thing I know – bang! – he's hit the ball 290 yards.

'Ready when you are, Mr Trevino,' said camera one.

'He's already hit it!' I told the crew.

'While he was still talking?'

'Yes, and I swear while he wasn't even looking!'

We had a good day in bad weather … well, actually Sandy did. Apart from chipping from nowhere, hitting the flag at 100 mph and stopping dead for a four-inch putt, I did very little to help our win by four shots.

Lee Trevino was brilliant both with club and repartee while Tarby was also his usual entertaining self, and quite a wizard with the golf shot. On the day, however, Sandy was outstanding – he missed nothing! 'I can't be as funny as Lee,' he told me. 'Don't worry,' I replied. 'I'll do the funnies. You just keep playing out of your skin,' And he did.

The day remains a great memory of trepidation followed by exhilaration. How much we can receive when we dedicate ourselves to the 'great game'. It is truly a wonderful leveller, a marvellous soother of aches of all sorts, and a friend when all else seems lost.

There have been happier TV days for me – notably the time I was the victim for a Noel Edmonds's Gotcha Oscar.

What a set-up that was: it included my management team, my wife, my entire family – all involved in a ploy to hatch a plot to catch a poor unsuspecting comic.

I was working on a tour of Butlin's Holiday Worlds in 1991, travelling up to 1500 miles a week, enough to guarantee to soften the brain and burn out the car. During this run I was told by Tom and Kevin, my managers, that I had been chosen to help present a TV show on the history of golf. Keith Chegwin was to be the interviewer. I would be playing in 1920s get-up, including period cap and clubs, and comment, as I went along, on how it felt using all this vintage gear.

After a journey from Minehead to Ealing, with little

sleep, I was wide open to be picked on. Togged up in this 1920s costume, a stiff collar, studless shoes, plus fours and a monster cap reminiscent of the type the late Colin Crompton used to wear when hosting the Wheeltappers and Shunters Social Club, I strode out on to the first to be greeted by a normal-looking film crew. I chose a three-wood from a very old bag full of very old clubs, while trying to keep calm and 'start off with a good 'un'.

Almost immediately I found myself the centre of harassment. The sound man kept interrupting and walking into my line of fire. Cheggers dropped the golf bag behind me and talked all through my backswing.

Whack! I pulled the drive. It was no good for the film. 'Reload.'

I was unhappy with the club-face, and decided it was not as square as it could be. This was confirmed when – whack! I duffed the next shot into a bunker. 'Reload!'

I was beginning to suspect the clubs, and changed the three-wood for a five. One good swing and – whack! This time we were off down the fairway, 220 yards or more. I decided the clubs were all right and began to relax.

While lining up the second shot and talking it through with Cheggers, Noel moved in back of me, heavily disguised, and as I swung he let off with both barrels of a shotgun at 'rabbits' in the shubbery.

'Golly heck,' I cried (or words to that effect). Suddenly I realised that the bushes he aimed at weren't moving. Could he be firing blanks? But why? Perhaps it was a wind-up. If it wasn't Noel Edmonds, it might be Jeremy Beadle. In any event I decided to play along.

Once I had sussed it, the result was great fun. They did their best to wind me up with duff advice, brought on noisy motorbikes, tractors – finally I was introduced to a 'Mr Heaney' who ostensibly owned a priceless golf ball which he brought out in a special wooden presentation box. Cheggers told me he was going to 'lend it to us for you to putt with'.

The gag was the ball would go into the hole in which there was a trick flap. The ball dropped down, the flap came up and to all intents and purposes the hole appeared empty, the ball having disappeared. Good gag!

Twice I missed the putt, infuriating for the crew, but the third time I sank it and 'Mr Heaney' went raving bonkers looking for his ball. On came Noel again, still in disguise, to join in the argument.

I decided to keep out of it while the heated confab went on, and chose my moment to intervene.

'Excuse me, Noel,' I said, 'it's like this …' And the penny dropped all round.

The 'Gotcha Oscar' now stands in my snooker room as a memento of an unforgettable day – it looked good on telly too. I was very thankful to Noel, and to the rest of the team, for thinking of me.

TV is a great source of memories, but there have been times when I've wished I had a full blown crew, or even a camera, to record an event for posterity.

My mind goes back to a day at one of my favourite clubs, Penwortham near Preston. Over the years it has remained a club dear to my heart: the members, its secretary and the committee are all a great bunch.

Many a game I have played there – and many a 'megameal' I have attempted! Joe, the steward, made the largest mixed grills in the world. Fry a dozen eggs, four pounds of sausages, one cow, one pig … only joking! But only just.

It was Thursday morning in July and a pal and I had arrived to play a quick 18 holes. John, the Penwortham secretary, had organised coffees and I had a brandy as a 'heart starter'. Then it rained heavily.

Discretion being the better part of valour, we decided to have another coffee and debate our prospects.

Eventually the consensus was that we'd stay in the warm: no use catching cold.

That's when they started arriving ... the Society, booked in for the full day. Thirty-six able-looking men who made much noise with their carefree banter and various modes of limbering up, none of which would have been recommended by Jane Fonda.

The first at Penwortham is a good par four, trees and trouble all down the left but nothing that a steady tee shot can't handle. From the clubhouse we watched 36 golfers tee off and counted them out. Unbelievably, only one player hit the fairway and that was with his second.

There should have been cameras that day! We were witnessing the worst collective group of golfers ever.

We watched them out of sight and sighed. Half an hour later a two-ball strode out on to the first and played the hole beautifully. Obviously low handicappers and used to the course.

Suddenly our minds raced fast forward. What would happen when this two-ball caught up with the rear of the Society? They will be thinking, 'We'll just get through these three and we'll be clear ...' Wait until they find they're behind twelve threesomes, all just as bad as each other! Welcome to my nightmare ...

Ah yes, the funny side of golf ... you can't beat it, you can join it, or you can have just as much fun watching it.

Who was the man in the crowd? He'll probably be forever anonymous, but for all that he'll be forever in my thoughts.

Witness Royal Birkdale, hosting the British Open in 1976. I had only recently become interested in the game and was watching Jack Nicklaus on the tee, hammering a ball out of sight down the first. 'Rubbish,' said a voice, quite distinctly in the crowd. 'His tee never went backwards!'

If it is unwise to open your mouth in the gallery, it is

COUGH
MIX

also unwise to be unwell. I recall a charity game at Torquay, and a very gentle-mannered celebrity on the tee, struggling not only with his shot but with a cougher in the crowd.

The golfer addressed the ball – Cough! He relaxed and addressed it again – Cough!

And so on. Eventually the quiet man of golf stared hard at the unhealthy fan. Silence fell and he played his shot. As he left the tee the quiet man turned to the unhealthy fan and said, 'You know that stare I gave you – I really meant it!' That was telling him!

If you are talking golf or talking about golf, you must know what you're saying. And if you are in any doubt, check with my dad – he knows!

Remember the controversy over the simple pronunciation of one player's name? The television commentators couldn't decide: was it 'Ola-tha-bal' or 'Olazz-abal', and which syllables should be stressed?

No one knew for sure until my dad said to me: 'That Josie Ozzleball is good, in'ne?'

Now we know. And yes, dad, he is good. I played with Jose in the Benson & Hedges – what a player. He has a great temperament and is a real gentleman. I'm a big Ozzleball fan.

ELEVENTH HOLE

Home and Away

PLAYING overseas and in unaccustomed circumstances can be a pleasure, but it can also throw up hazards all its own. There are compensations ... the sun on your back, beautifully manicured greens, fairways like a front lawn. Nothing like it!

Each year Pat and I take a welcome break and work two or three weeks for P&O aboard one of their world cruise liners, among which I claim the *Canberra* as my favourite. If ever a man had a love affair with a ship, 'twas she and me!

Acapulco is one of the main ports of call on one leg of this cruise and I have been lucky enough to visit it many times. The Princess Hotel is an elegant residence and I have played the beautiful course there on two occasions. On the first time out, accompanied by the ship's purser and two fellow entertainers, it was an idyllic day, with steady scores and easy on the feet – even the girls enjoyed the walk.

I only hit trouble once, and hit a 'shot of shots' to escape – in front of witnesses too! I'd driven a three-wood to the right. It went a long way but landed behind a tallish tree, maybe 15 feet back. A direct line to the green was blocked and I approached the ball with thinking cap in overdrive.

Out from a neighbouring condominium came a huge man, and I'm talking gross weight here! Seriously, he must have been 30 stones – at least he would have been in the UK. But as he was American, I shudder to think how many pounds he weighed.

Although only in his mid-30s, or possibly younger if his charming wife was any guide, he wheezed and lumbered like an old 'un. Oh, the penalties of being too overweight.

'Hi, young feller,' he called.

'My kind of bloke!' I thought, suddenly feeling a lot less than my 45 years.

'What do you plan doing with this shot?' he asked me.

'Tell me what the great Tom Watson would do,' I suggested.

'Well,' said 'my kind of bloke'. 'I guess he'd tickle a little three-iron off his back foot, draw it low around the tree and stiff it by the flag.'

Three-iron, back foot, swing and duck in case of the rebound, Tom – Whoosh! The ball flew like a bullet, drew round the tree and landed a foot from the stick. A dream of a shot!

'Remember,' I said to myself, 'keep cool, look disappointed, move away quickly ...' I did.

'Gee, did you see that, Martha? He didn't like it! I tell you, I've seen some golf in my day, but ...'

Keep talking pal, I ponder as I walk to the green. I can't stop now, I'm on a roll. Please God, the putt drops ... and it did!

Another year, another cruise, and Pat and are back in Acapulco, playing the Princess again in company with a fellow artiste called Neville, plus Joe O'Keefe, a retired Irish Army commandant, and Sam, a passenger of dubious credentials. We later decided he was probably a spy, but we didn't know for which side.

If you ever play the Princess course, take a tip from me. Don't listen to wifely advice!

'Why don't we hire a buggy and I'll drive us?' suggested Pat.

Bearing in mind that I usually play golf for exercise, I should have insisted on carrying my bag, but on this day I gave in. We hired two buggies and set off in convoy to 'murder this course'. The problem with hiring a buggy, of course, is that you are never away from the ball. You have hardly hit it before you are beside it again. The buggy ride gives little time for thought and no conception of distance played.

The final drawback is the drinks buggy full of gin, tonic and ice which tends to dog you on courses like the Princess – and always serves large measures.

So it was that we partook of the devil's brew while playing the angels' game. The effect of cool gin in a hot climate is to make golf seem a very easy game, and adversaries are prone to come out with such friendly sympathetic comments.

A totally duffed tee shot brings, 'Not easy from there', and indifferent strokes all the way round are accompanied by, 'Good shot!' 'Bravo!' 'Well done!'

The truth is that too much of the falling down liquid can let you down just when you don't expect it.

There is a par four at Acapulco, easy enough on paper, with only two hazards of any note. In front of the tee is a lake, biggish, but nothing a seven-iron can't carry, and further up the fairway is a huge tree, impressive but no threat to the hole.

Playing last of the four that day, I watched my three 'chums' play successive shots straight into the lake. Three drives, three dives. Spectators were gathering to watch the course record being broken.

'You've got to do something to save face, Tom,' was the spluttered advice from the erstwhile pals, so I did some thinking, albeit scrambled.

'Three-wood for safety, easy swing, watch the right

shoulder doesn't lurch through and smother the shot … head still, relax … slow take away …' When in doubt remember a tip I learned from a little old lady: 'Sing "Nellie the Elephant" to yourself for tempo!' (Mind you, it depends on how fast you sing it …)

All this procedure was put into practice; after all I was saving face on behalf of the whole of P&O. The ball flew sweet as a bird, over the lake, heading for the fairway.

Then the little pilot inside the ball did the unforgivable. He steered the thing to the left. Was it the gin? Did I breathe unfairly on the ball before teeing off?

Whatever the reason, my drive hit the tree front and centre, and, amidst screams of laughter and gurgles from the gallery, it ricocheted straight back into the lake. Four drives, four dives – an unbeatable record for that hole.

Then there was Kagoshima, Japan, a beautiful port and equally beautiful people, willing to show us around their city, and even their homes. When time came for us to leave, a huge choir of Japanese school children congregated at midnight on a cool evening, dressed in their uniforms and carrying candles, to sing 'Auld Lang Syne' in conjunction with a tannoyed record.

In the background tugs were hooting, and the *Canberra* was echoing their tribute while thousands of passengers sang, waved and cheered. Twenty minutes later, the novelty was beginning wear off. The children were beginning to shiver, the tannoy wavering and the waves from the passengers weaker as the cheers died away. Something was obviously wrong, but no – ten more minutes, and we began to inch away from the quay. 'Auld Lang Syne' came back to full strength and there was one last burst of spontaneous enjoyment.

But what caused the hiccup in the proceedings? The answer was Reg the Veg!

Reg was in charge of peeling vegetables and getting rid of the waste, which was usually bagged and weighted, then dumped at sea without trace. But not in Kagoshima.

Reg had decided to unload in the docks, so swung a surreptitious sack out from the ship's loading bay – and forgot to let go. Out he went, landing with the sack between the ship and the quay. Panic ensued. Dockers tried to hold off the ship with poles, while some wag shouted 'Shark!' Reg popped out in a trice!

Back on board he was asked for an explanation, in other words, 'What the blankety blank was going on?'

'It was like this,' explained Reg, 'I swung the sack out of the loading bay and … argh!' And out he flew again, repeating the operation as before, keeping thousands waiting while he was rescued a second time.

With the ship back at sea, I was to be found in the golf practice nets, naturally. It was great for posing in front of Japanese tourists! My swing must be on dozens of Japanese home video films … goodness knows what they think of the hacker in the long shorts, flip-flops, white body and red head. I must look like a golfing safety match.

The *Canberra* is certainly a very special cruise ship, and, as with golf, when you are on her the years just roll away. I well recall bidding farewell to her in 1982, in the midst of the Falklands War. The whole crew volunteered for active service and I left the ship at Southampton. Hours later she was being re-equipped for the hostilities, a big white target in the South Atlantic. Thankfully she returned intact.

I know the old saying that you make your own luck … 'The more you practise, the luckier you get, etc.' But I think my personal luck changes for the worse whenever I leave British shores.

Take Spain, home of great golfers, great courses, and beautiful weather – most of the time. Why can't I play well there? Maybe there is too much going for the golfer, no big worries or challenges. At least that's my pretty weak excuse.

Aloha golf course is a gem of a spot, with manicured fairways and greens, super company, very good, steady players. Here, one summer, I spent five days playing goodish golf, preferring early mornings when the greens were still damp with dew and easier to putt on than later in the day when they were like glass.

Kenny Lynch was a great partner on a couple of occasions, and so was a Geordie lad, a smashing character called Dan McKenzie. After a couple of days of blissful friendly games I was approached to play in a Celebrity-Am day for charity. All the lads were there – Tarby, Kenny, Kevin Keegan and so on. Of course I said I would take part: 'I'd be delighted, can't wait, hold me back, sure thing ...' and all that. But wait a minute ...

I am picked to partner a chap who was over 75 at least. I decided it's no problem. There is good news – he plays off 28. Bad news – handicaps are only allowed up to 18. Even worse news – he can't carry a bag.

Good news – I'll hire a buggy. Bad news – all the buggies are accounted for.

Good news – I'll get a caddie. Bad news – 'Sorry señor, the caddies, they are all busy.'

So I have to hump the gear for both of us.

It wouldn't have been so bad if we'd kept our drives together but no way! I must have walked double the length of Aloha that day, feeling like a cross between Gunga Din and a pack-horse. In the end, the score became secondary to actually staying alive in the heat. I was delighted to break 100 and not break my back. The clubhouse loomed like a friendly oasis and the first three ice-cold lagers never touched the sides ...

Who cares who won the money that day – I reckoned I'd found a new endurance test for the SAS!

But what of Dan McKenzie? He was a builder, a good

A new endurance test for the SAS

golfer and splendid company, whom I met on my first day at Aloha. He has a place out there and speaks Spanish fluently. In fact, being a Geordie, he speaks Spanish better than English.

He and his lovely wife royally entertained Pat and me both on and off the course, and I must relate one lovely anecdote which to me typifies the Geordie wit.

We went for a meal one night in Porto Buenos. The meal was enormous, but then so was the bill. It was too big, we reckoned, by about £60 or its Spanish equivalent.

'This bill's not right,' said Dan to the waiter.

'Que?' said Manuel's double.

'The bill is wrong,' persisted Dan. 'Bring the manager.'

Bearing in mind that while the waiters conversed, Dan could understand every word they said, he was ready when the manager arrived.

'Can I help you, señor?'

'Aye. This bill is not right. The bill is erroneous.' If the manager looked confused, I must admit Dan had me with that one too.

'We will have to negotiate this bill,' Dan told him.

'Negotiate? I do not understand, señor.'

'It's quite simple,' said our genial Geordie. 'You see this total at the bottom? This is what you're not getting!'

Ah, the logic of simplicity. I must catch up with Dan and his mates the next time I'm on the Costa del Sol.

Talking of home and away, it reminds me that in golf, as in life, the unexpected can hit you right between the eyes at the most unlikely moment.

I remember Castletown Links on the Isle of Man, a good course, tricky on any day, difficult in the wind. The sort of course that makes you smile if you can keep within four of your handicap.

I have played Castletown on many occasions, and lost a few balls to the Irish Sea. I have met great companions there and shared their laughter. But once, just once, it was the scene of my worst ever golf day. Believe me, I have had a few bad 'uns, but this was the ultimate!

It all started miles away in Panama City … I've always said if you're going to the Isle of Man you should start in South America.

Pat and I were leaving the *Canberra* at Cristóbal, the port nearest to the Panama Canal. We'd had a great cruise, and finished off with a very long night entertaining the crew. As I recall, I was still playing my guitar at 5.30 am and at several different times through the night, for no reason at all, poured cold lager over my head to stay awake.

We crashed out in our cabin at about 6 am and had hardly settled when the door opened and a chap in full chef's uniform wheeled in a silver salver on a trolley saying, 'Your order, sir!'

My God, where was I? What had I ordered? Normally when I'm in jolly vein I order Lobster Thermidor but hopefully not this time! Instead it was a full English breakfast – bacon, runny eggs, the works. Then I noticed the 'chef's' eyes: they were bloodshot. And I looked at the clock; it was 7 am. I knew then it was a wind-up. The 'chef' hadn't been to bed yet.

Never mind, the food was welcome. We ate heartily, then couldn't get back to sleep. Now we had to spend several hours wandering ashore before our flight home. But so what? Plenty of time to recover before I worked again …

The *Canberra* sailed off into the mist leaving Pat and me to face the rigours of the airport. The plane, it appeared, was not air-worthy and there would be a delay of fully 24 hours before it could be fixed. The alternative was a full week's wait before the next flight.

Nobody slept that night. We all just ambled zombie-like around the hotel in the steamy evening, wondering, just wondering. The next day at the airport – no joy, no plane! What now?

Out of the blue came our saviour, an amazing chap called Major Peter Ball, a retired army man and an absolute wizard at organisation. He tackled the airport staff. 'Bring me the highest ranking person here who can speak English!' They did.

'Bring me an A-Z of flights.' They did.

'I want three seats on the next plane going east, first class, mind. And a taxi to take us back to the hotel where you will ensure we are re-accommodated.' They did.

Next morning, we took an Iberian flight to Madrid to link up with a BA flight to Heathrow, eternally grateful to the major. There was just time to unpack, repack and fly off to an after-dinner job on the Isle of Man. In three days we had had barely three and a half hours' sleep. My head was still banging, my fingers still raw from guitar strumming, my throat aching. Never mind, I reasoned, we can sleep all day at Castletown, take a shower, have a shave and a Strepsil and still be on about 11 pm for an hour.

It was not to be. We tottered off the plane at Ronaldsway and fell into a cab. At Castletown we checked in, went up to the bedroom and dropped into bed.

Then the phone rang. 'Who knows I'm here?' I thought, 'Must be a wrong number. Ignore it.' But it kept ringing so I eventually answered it and it was the organiser of the 'do' at which I was due to speak.

'Where are you?' he demanded. 'We're waiting for you on the first tee. Hurry on down!'

'Sorry,' I said, 'I haven't brought my clubs.' No problem, they had a set they could lend me.

'No shoes?' What size, he asked. We'll find a pair.

Drat and double drat! There was no escape …

I staggered around the bedroom, bumping into almost everything, to make myself almost presentable – eye drops, breath freshener, after shave. Breathe in, shoulders back …

'I don't know how you can do it,' said Pat. 'You're so brave!' Nice words but they didn't cure my ills. So I ventured out into the breeze, all of 40 mph off the sea.

I do not believe I could have played a worse 18 holes if it had been pitch dark and myself handcuffed. 'Dreadful' would have been praise. 'Stinker' was nearer the truth.

Never will I forget one passing player, the third four to come through as I searched the countryside for my ball. He turned to his partner and remarked: 'Single figures and he plays like that! God knows how bad his jokes will be!'

Luckily they were better than we all thought possible. In truth I wowed the late night crowd, more by good luck than skill. But I reckon that round of golf shortened my life by a full three years.

Why can't we keep our heads together and learn that life is a marathon and not a sprint? The ideal is to stay as fit as possible, and ration the good times. No need to cram everything into today. Well, up to a point.

Remember the story of the American billionaire who was so afraid of a nuclear holocaust that he spent millions of dollars building a fall-out shelter in the Nevada desert. He was just putting the last brick in the wall when an Indian shot him in the back with an arrow. So you see, you never know …

TWELFTH HOLE

Preparation and Practice

OH, HOW LUCKY I've been – to do a job I really enjoy and get well paid for being myself. No acting, no rehearsing.

Along with that, how lucky to have a hobby I enjoy as much as life itself. What more could a comic ask for? Well, good health and good friends, I guess, but then I have been amply blessed in those departments too.

From my early days as a singer in Liverpool pubs, teaching all day, singing all night and sleeping in shifts, it became quickly apparent that health and relaxation were vital to the job. It was no use spending the whole night carousing and then spend all the next day recovering … you know the sort of thing, eight paracetamols, mega-cups of Alka Seltzer, port and brandy to settle the stomach … It's no use dreading going on again the following night because your head's not together.

It is more important to keep both body and head as fit as possible, while regularly honing the act, introducing new material and dropping the dead wood. You have to work at this job day after day.

I began by making notes in the working men's clubs. I bought a large 'page a day' diary and at a venue I would list the names of the doorman, the secretary, compère and all the people with whom I had direct contact. The next time it was easy to walk in and say, 'Hello Charlie. How's the wife's hip?' and get them to think, 'Blimey, he's remembered! What a nice guy!'

Another sharp move was to say to each concert secretary or booker, when they began complimenting me on my act, 'My agent doesn't know how good I am. No one ever tells him!'

That way I had my agent bombarded with complimentary letters and phone calls about me.

But most important of all, as I entered a new piece of comedy into the act, I would also note the date. This meant that at any time I could go back to a venue and have a list of all the material they hadn't heard before.

The only pitfall on the way was ignorance of new technology. I entered all the new material and dates I had carefully collated on to a computer disc. Then my son Stephen decided to use a microwave next to the computer and the 'wave spill' wiped the disc! It took me several days checking through envelopes, Woodbine packets and serviettes to recoup the details.

Still the system is tight now and works virtually all the time, given normal circumstances – mike, lights, audience still awake …

This strategy, believe it or not, has also helped to improve my golf, or at least prevent the worst aspects of my game recurring.

One of the earliest lessons I learned came from a smashing newspaper strip, and was from Gary Player, that golfing legend and bunker player par excellence. 'Always accept your punishment with the same eagerness you accept good luck,' he wrote. And how right that is.

Come on – how many times have we duffed a drive into the trees, and ended up blocked out to the green except for a possible needle-eyed gap ahead. All sense says, 'Play safe to the fairway and forgo a shot', but the devil inside you is saying, 'Go for the gap. The pros would!' They probably wouldn't, you know.

Here's another great line that little devil throws at you: 'Don't forget all trees are basically 90 per cent water!' Oh really? When was the last time you hit a tree and heard a splash!

How many good looking cards have been ruined by that totally over-ambitious shot. You've probably been there: it's a par five dog-leg, and the simple way is a three-wood, middle iron, wedge, and one or two putts – a safe par. Sounds so sensible one can feel the serenity and lack of pressure.

Contrast that to the actual situation, standing on the tee and listening to 'you know who'. The devilish voice is saying, 'Blast the driver hard as you can, smash a three-wood and we're on in two. Who knows – you could even be near the pin. Down for three or at worst four. Go on!' Hard to resist, isn't it?

Consistency will never come from a rush of blood, so why not be practical and face facts? The secret of consistency is knowing what you can't do, and never trying it. That's probably incorrect grammatically, but it's right enough in golf terms!

While on tour I like to make good use of driving ranges, which are becoming more and more popular. In Brighouse, West Yorkshire, for instance, there's a beautiful council-owned driving range. The golf shop is attached to a small municipal course, all the equipment is in good repair, and it is floodlit – this obviously has to be the thing of the future if golf takes on the same value here as it has in, say, Japan, where they have multi-storey driving ranges. You have to possess a very good eye to determine which ball is actually yours, I guess, but it gives the Japanese something to do when there are so few golf courses.

Driving ranges are ideal for the likes of me. When I can't afford the time for a full round of golf I can spend a couple of hours knocking buckets of balls on the range. In fact it was at a driving range where I first had lessons to play golf properly. I have received lessons from various pros on my travels, but the major problem is that in order to go out and practise, you need a lot of grass, a lot of space between you and where you are actually knocking the ball, a lot of practice balls and a lot of time. At a driving range you just smack 'em into the distance and hours later a man picks 'em up in a machine! Can't be bad.

Another good thing about being at home on a range is that when you stand in your 'box' you are square on – everything is lined up, the angles are right, and when you hit the ball you know exactly where it should go. It is a totally different feel to smacking one down a fairway and when you look up, the green is somewhere in the distance and all around is open space and wilderness.

Golfing ranges are therefore very handy to practise golf theory. And one of the great things I was taught on the range was to take the club-head away from the ball with my left hand – in fact, to make everything left-handed. You learn to put the club-face down with your left hand, with the blade facing in the direction you want to hit the ball, to stand square to the blade of the club and place your right hand to the club. In taking the club away you start with your left hand, which doesn't lurch it away but gives it a nice gentle swing, and this makes sure that when the club is taken away and the shoulder is turned, the head will come back in the same line to the ball. So you are not tempted into having a thrash, with your right shoulder coming in and trying to smash the ball with your right hand.

One of the first rules of golf, as far as I am concerned, is that you learn to play a golf stroke instead of a golf hit when you swing the club. As always, the major guiding principle is tempo. It doesn't matter how well you swing or how well in line everything is, if you swing at 150 mph, your chances of returning the club-head to the ball at the same angle as it left it are virtually nil, because everything happens in such a blur of speed and anything could result. Your hands, your wrists, your ankles, your eyes, your head could move. I am not saying we should all swing at a funereal pace but it should be a gentle swing.

Think tempo – and think in terms of allowing the club-head to come away from the ball so that you can see its path, if need be, thus giving the body time to turn, because weight has to transfer from left foot to right foot and then back again. And remember, of course, that the most important six inches of any golf swing are the three inches just as you hit the ball and the three inches just after you've hit the ball as the club-head goes through it. That's the only point of the club swing that actually propels the ball. Anything that goes on behind your back or over your shoulder or above your head when you've finished is only frills. The essential moment is when the blade actually hits the ball and guides it away to the target.

The most important thing in golf, next to your swing when trying to hit a ball, is complete concentration. The really vital part of any golfer, so it is said, is the bit between the ears. If you don't think you are going to play well, then you won't play well.

I remember a pro telling me that he kept changing his putter. 'I am never happy with a putter for a long time. I might change it once a fortnight or once every three weeks. I have a wardrobe full of putters at home.' A fairly new putter that impressed him might not guarantee him

A mental blind spot when it comes to left and right

holing every putt but it would give him the confidence to expect to hole every putt. Once that confidence had gone and he began to believe he was not going to hole putts with it, he would have to change it.

So a lot of the art of golf is in the mind, convincing yourself that your swing is right and that your choice of club is right. It is no good selecting a club from your golf bag and then thinking, 'I'm sure I should have picked another one.' Select a club, stick with it and hit with it – try not to smash it or be too gentle with it to compensate for selecting the 'wrong' club. Hit it quite normally, never stopping halfway through to say to yourself, 'This isn't going to work. I should never have picked an eight-iron'. As soon as you do that you are bound to duff the shot. You are thinking wrong, you're thinking anti-golf, you're resorting to power instead of technique, and you are 99 per cent certain to play a bad shot.

To be a good golfer, it helps to know right from left – or at least be aware of the difference. It is amazing how many people have a mental blind spot in this area. My Pat still uses 'knife side' and 'fork side'!

If you are a right-handed person then golf is naturally a left-sided game. I think the nicest image of golf was given by a young assistant pro who said to me, 'There are mornings when I get up and I can see the picture. I can put the club-head to the ball and I can see where the ball is going to go, whether it is going away or coming back, flying to this point or that point ... the picture is clear. If you can't visualise that picture then you can't play the shot.' And he was right. It is all a matter of composure and minimising the drawbacks.

It is fun to watch an opponent stagger into a pot bunker wielding a two-wood and it's great to be able to sympathise when he hits the face of the trap and buries himself deeper in the mire.

'Hard luck – two inches higher and you'd have been on

the green.' Hopefully that will convince him to try the shot again if he finds himself in another trap.

Sometimes preparation for the game can include practising those extremely important comments on your opponent's game, and then getting the timing right.

I learnt from some great teachers ... 'On your back swing are you breathing out or breathing in?' That's a cracker!

Cardew 'The Cad' Robinson takes the blame for the next beauty. He never did it to me, but I have it on good authority that he sometimes lets his opponent play two or three good holes and then says, 'Now that last shot, you got everything right – arms, hands, legs, balance ...'

The poor victim then spends the rest of the round trying to get 'everything right' again – and failing, naturally. It's another version of the 'gotcha' joke. If you don't know the 'gotcha' story, ask around!

I suppose the words about golf that have had the most lasting effect on me came from Gil Dova, my American friend, a golf fanatic whose greatest moment, he says, was actually dreaming he'd won the US Open. He could even remember the exact score on each hole. What a disappointment waking up must have been!

Gil said to me, 'The greatest thing about golf is the pride it gives you in your own ability. Shame alone prevents people giving wrong handicaps in order to win.'

And you know, all joking aside, that is true of most golfers. All right, there are bandits in the game and we get to know them over the years. But generally, if anything, the handicap system works for us and against us because we are always trying to be better than we are.

The handicap system, after all, is probably the reason why golf is the only game in which you and I, scratch or 28 handicap, can take on the world's best and have half a chance.

There is no way you could take on a tennis player, even

with three points start in each game. Or match a world class boxer even with one hand tied behind his back. Or a snooker pro, even with a four blacks start.

Yet play golf with a great player, he off the back tees and giving you shots, and who knows? The one sure thing is that the pro will be as helpful to you as possible, giving any advice that will help you improve your game. That's golf – a game for the fairest of the fair.

It is pride in personal ability that is the key to preparing and playing well. Winning really becomes secondary. Wouldn't you prefer to be six under par and lose than be ten over and win?

I recall the story of the old codger who at 75 had given a lifetime's leisure to playing a hacker's game at his local club. On the eve of his 76th birthday he was asked by the club captain what his one main ambition was.

'I've always dreamed of reducing my handicap to 27,' he mused.

'Aha …' thought the captain. 'Maybe, just maybe …'

On the morn of his 76th birthday, the old codger shuffled out of the car park into the clubhouse to be greeted by the chairman of the handicap committee.

'I'm sorry, Harry,' he tells him, 'but after much deliberation and observation, we have to say that we've decided to cut you to 27.'

'Yippee,' came the answer as Harry did an Irish jig and rushed to the bar for a celebratory drink.

After that a delirious Harry joined three lifelong chums for a birthday round of golf, all full of the joys of spring. Three hours later they trudged back in, heads down and wheezing.

'How'd it go, Harry?' asked the skipper.

'Rubbish,' said Harry. 'I played like a 28!'

THIRTEENTH HOLE

I'm Enjoying It, Honest ...

WHAT IS THE classic chauvinistic golf gag? 'I'll never forget my wedding day. I holed a 32 ft putt.'

I suppose in all walks of life there are things that make unforgettable impressions, but only in the great game are there so many, many things ...

Enjoyment, the main reason for playing golf, so they say, can be achieved through good performance or good results. Preparation, that vital cog in the performance wheel, is all – plus natural talent as well.

Witness the would-be golfer given this advice by the golf pro who said, 'If I were you, I'd go down the driving range, spend about three hours hitting about 200 golf balls and then pack up altogether ...'

Never dismiss the flippant golf gag. There could just be a glimmer of truth in it.

'Our club never play away matches 'cos the captain hasn't got a tie.'

'Ours is the only club where the putting green is cobbled.'

'I had to take up golf otherwise I'd never see my doctor.'

'Charlie says he's going to drown himself. What do you think?'

'No chance – he can't keep his head down long enough.'

'I'll tell you how bad our team was – we were only

together on the tee. We were scattered around the course like shrapnel.'

Yes, all good stuff … and more to come, because in golf who knows what will happen next?

Two lifelong adversaries are out on a Sunday morning, scores level and more than 50p riding on the game.

Player A is in the semi-rough and not sitting too well.

'Three-wood, caddie.' Addresses ball – no.

'Five-wood, caddie.' Addresses ball again, jiggles club – no.

'Three-wood again.' Another jiggle.

'Five-wood again.' Jiggle, jiggle.

'Hmm. I don't think this is a wood shot …'

Player B chips in, 'No, but it soon will be!'

Then there is the expert ball marker – you must have met him. This fellow is more deft at sleight of hand than Paul Daniels.

Instead of marking behind the ball, he marks in front. Then, when replacing the ball, he puts it in front of the marker.

I watched one from close up one day and a member of our four said, 'Careful, pal. If you mark that ball once more, you'll be in the hole.'

See? There's fun even in adversity on a golf course. Surely those stories we pass on at golf dinners aren't all jokes …

'The way he played he didn't need a watch. He needed a compass.'

'A bloke with us cried "Fore!" and an auctioneer in the game ahead said, 'Do I hear four-fifty?'

'Did you hear about the bloke who won the Irish Open two up and six to play?'

What about the almighty row coming from the 18th green, lots of screaming, shouting and scuffling. 'What's going on?' asks the steward, sprinting towards the incident.

The other three saw a hand rise as if to grasp Excalibur

'My mate's just had a stroke,' said the player, 'and these two are trying to count it!' Ugh! Even I don't believe that one!

Although there was the tale of the three who came in saying, 'Poor old Percy passed away on the seventh green.'

'Oh dear,' said the steward. 'You must have been devastated.'

'Yes – particularly as we've had to carry him for 11 holes.'

If golf jokes are often a little macabre, they still show a healthy ability to poke fun at ourselves and our passion for the game.

Witness the bloke whose ball flew into a lake, infuriating him so much that he stormed in after it, his head gradually disappearing under the water, leaving only a floating cap.

After an interminable wait, the other three saw a hand rise as if grasping Excalibur and flicker gently.

'He's drowning for sure,' says one.

'Not necessarily,' says his partner. 'He could be calling for a five-iron.'

Then there is the bloke whose misfortune is to partner a fussy putter. You've all met this one – he stalks the hole for fully 20 minutes, looking for borrows, holding up the putter and aligning the head behind it. What are they looking for?

'When was this green cut, caddie?'

'This morning, sir.'

'Yes, but what time this morning?'

He's the one who finishes a foot from the hole and waits a while before saying, 'I didn't hear anything …' No, and you won't, pal!

The first time I ever played an American was at the Foxhills, Chertsey course, and I found myself teeing up with a Texas magician, Jay, over here on tour and appearing in my TV series. He asked, 'Would you like to join me for a knock?' and of course I was delighted to accept.

The first hole was no problem for me. I played a nice easy three-wood down the middle just to show Jay the line. On the tee Jay took his driver and – whack! Goodbye ball. Reload.

'Oops, Tommy,' he said. 'I'll just play a Mulligan.'

OK, I thought. It's transatlantic good will, hands across the sea, Anglo-American relations stuff … all good reasons for allowing him a free ball.

He took the same driver and – whack! – same result. Reload.

'Oops, Tommy,' he said. 'I'll just play a Shapiro.'

'Shapiro?' I ask.

'Jewish Mulligan, son.'

There was no answer to that, other than to bite the bullet, and keep your head down. Jay won, by the way.

Another day, another course, this time Shawhill in Lancashire – a great club, with a hotel and a golf complex that's popular with societies and ideal for corporate days – and I'm not just saying that because I happen to be a vice-president …

Anyhow, I recall one particular morning when, being the celebrity guest, it was my brief to play a hole with each team, present the prizes and perform the cabaret. It makes for a long day but it can be very satisfying.

The first at Shawhill is a good par four. There's trouble to the left and right but only if you go looking for it. Legends abound that the hole is drivable on a good day: 'Just catch the top of the rise in the right position and down she rolls.'

There is a slight dog-leg left, with trees on the right and general nasties on the left. To lead the way I played a good three-iron safe and slightly right of centre. The next two went slightly more right, the first into the undergrowth and the other, a man whose swing was so fast it was impossible to tell whether it was out to in or not, belted his to the left and, as far as I could tell, was lost forever.

While I was lining up the next shot for his friend, this player was crashing around looking for the lost ball on the left. Soon he cried, 'I've found it,' and a micro-second later – crump! – he'd smashed it out of Indian territory and as if by magic it plonked stiff by the pin. He was down for three the hard way.

We walked to the next hole where I had to wait for the next team, and I watched him assessing the hole. It's 142 yards, hardly any breeze and he took a two-wood.

'Look,' I said. 'It's never a two-wood from here. What did you use for your second on the last?'

'Five-iron,' he answered.

'Go for that, then,' I suggested.

He hit the five-iron as sweet as a nut and the ball had hole in one written all over it. One bounce and it disappeared into the hole for an eagle.

'What a start to a round,' I remarked.

'Better than that,' he beamed, 'I get a shot a hole as well.'

The last I saw of that team they were still trying to work out their partner's points to date. Surely I had just left the ultimate winner of the competition, but no! It transpired that after he left me he had tried to protect his gains and wrecked his card. So there is a God after all …

The 18th at Torquay (mentioned already in memory of the late, great Ted Ray) is a good-looking hole. It sweeps gently left to right, past the clubhouse, across the first fairway and the hole nestles by a wall below a school playground. It's amazing how far the noise of children playing can travel on a clear day.

Just to the right of the green is the practice ground, but not so you'd notice, unless you knew it was there.

A visiting celebrity, who shall be nameless, was doing a Sunday concert at the theatre where I was in summer season, and asked for a knock on the Monday morning. So there we were, me down the fairway left of centre, and maybe a seven-iron from home, and he over by the trees to the right, safe enough but short of my ball.

Slowly I realised he was not making a bee-line for his ball. Instead he would pause, stoop, stand erect and move on. Then it dawned – he had found a ball! No one about – a pick up! And further along he found another one … and another. Boy, this must be a nest of 'em!

Only the laughter borne on the wind brought him back to reality. As he looked ahead, pockets stuffed with Pinnacles, Titleists, Dunlops, he saw the pro and a pupil in the practice area. They'd been hitting all those balls he'd been picking up! Laugh? Well, he had to – especially as the entire clubhouse had witnessed it all.

Remember the apocryphal story about the man who won the pools, moved to Southport to live and was persuaded by his wife to take up golf? Maybe you've heard it before, and maybe then it was set at another course, but anyway it's the one that goes like this …

He went to his local sports shop and said, 'I'm thinking of taking up golf so I'd like to buy some bats.'

'Certainly sir,' said the owner, and off went our hero to pay for his first round of Royal Birkdale, complete with a bag of bats and plenty of 'ammo'.

He proceeded to tear shreds out of the course, hitting everything but the ball and generally creating havoc.

Back in the clubhouse he ordered lunch and tucked in while the other members grumbled at the bar.

'It's absolutely disgraceful – the man's an idiot.' 'Quite so. He's destroying the place!' 'Someone should tell him.'

So a committee man was delegated. He strode over to the pools winner and said, 'I say, my man. I want to have a word with you. I'm responsible for the greens here.'

'That's good,' said our man. 'As it happens I want a word with you. These sprouts are awful!'

Not a true story, but a good one for all that.

There are plenty of rules in golf not printed in any book – experience is the only way to learn them. How to sabotage the game of a person who is taking unfair advantage, for example. You know the sort – the one who is forever watching your club selection or listening to your request from the caddie. The simple solution is to have numbered head covers on the irons and put them on the wrong clubs. Boy, that soon stops their gallop!

Another ploy is to ignore their constant cries for relief from various lies. 'Is that a rabbit scraping?'

'Not unless he's got feet the size of a yeti!'

'Is there a ruling on this water?'

'Yes, get wet or drop a shot.'

We had a regular at Royal Ascot whom we used to call Dracula. They had planted some baby trees and put stakes round them for protection. If a young tree is staked you can get a drop ball a club length or two away, so you don't damage the tree. And they called him Dracula because every time he got near a tree he would ask, 'Is this a stake?'

The usual answer was, 'No, it's a pork chop!'

He's now retired to the course in the sky where I suppose he is still appealing against something!

FOURTEENTH HOLE

Golf? What Is Golf?

GOLF IS like the high jump – you never actually beat the game – there will eventually come the point whether it's a round of 60 or 55 or 50 or whatever, when you realise you are never going to go round a golf course in none!

All you can do to improve your own particular game is to remember your mistakes and learn from them, discover what your limitations are and play to them. And try to do the good things consistently well.

If you want to play a half decent game of golf, find a good golf pro. Ask around, check them out and stick with the one you choose. What with tours and summer seasons, this has been impossible for me. But the advantage of staying with one pro is that he will develop your game – because you are not going to learn it all today or tomorrow or in two years – then gradually show you the good habits and iron out any faults.

It is important, too, to play with good partners, or against good opposition. Probably the best games of golf I have ever played have been with players far better than I will ever be. It forces you to concentrate! Rather than look a complete idiot, you are forced to think and play the best game you possible can.

Another prime lesson I've learned in playing golf is

consideration for others. At my late stage of taking up the game (and probably the same goes for most people who take up golf late) we do it to for enjoyment, exercise and companionship. So you can show consideration in a variety of small ways – by raking out bunkers, replacing pitch marks, replacing divots and the like.

Equally important is consideration for other people's emotions, bearing in mind we can all be nervous, frustrated, tired, hot tempered – all the things that golf is *not* about. Golf should have a calming influence. The last thing you want to do is to play a game that winds you up so that you end up banging your head against the wall and breaking your clubs. Golf must be played serenely. Henry Cotton once criticised a well-known pro for practising when he was tired, after doing an exhausting round of personal appearances and so on. We have to give golf our fullest attention when we play. It's no good steaming up to the club with two minutes to spare before you run on to the tee, slinging your shoes on and trying to smash the first ball 300 yards.

Golf is a way of life, a way of slowing you down, taking your mind off the problems of the day, helping you to relax in your own kind of company.

There are no short cuts. It's all down to serious effort and serious concentration – blood, sweat and tears, if you like – you only get out of golf what you put into it. If you play a fluffy shot, you get a fluffy result. If you concentrate on getting the correct weight of head through the ball at the right speed, you get the kind of shot that's as good as any pro could play – though you might not hit it so far.

You can get sentimentally attached to your equipment, sometimes to the detriment of your game. One girl who was a member at our club collected golf balls the way we used to collect conkers. She had one particular ball with which she had played 22 complete rounds of golf. It broke her heart when she lost it. I think she would have been happier if it had broken in half. At least she could have said, 'Well, that's it finished, I can't use it again.' Just knowing this favourite ball was out there somewhere, lost in the bushes – she was still pining for it weeks later!

I mentioned that John O'Neill has a putter which he has had ages and it is almost as bent as Harry Lauder's walking stick – yet it works for him. And that's as it should be. If it works, stick with it. If you think it's helping you, then that's 30 per cent of the job. But many golfers prefer to resort to alternatives. If something goes wrong and they three-putt three holes in a row, they will probably drag out another putter. Because golfers will never blame themselves – they will always blame the club. 'The putter's too light, too heavy, the face is gone, it's worn ... give me something new.' We're conning ourselves really.

Golfers also tend to have a weird selection of clubs in their bag. I would love to empty Trevino's bag and see what's in there. I know he has two different wedges. He may even have three, either to get the ball up or to get it up and knock it a long way as well. And apparently he has a couple of three-irons and a couple of three-woods. You and I buy a full set of clubs and we go out with one of each. The pros don't do that: they may have a couple of woods and one iron, or a couple of three irons and no two-iron. Because the pros can make one club do another club's job.

One of the most amazing things I saw was Sevvy playing a round of golf with only one club. He just used the four-iron – as a driver, a wedge and a putter – and still parred the course!

Pros can adjust their drivers too. Those I have picked are a lot heavier than you expect them to be because they have lead weights underneath them. The basic rule is if it works for you, use it.

I try to have a complete set of clubs of the same make. I

know guys who have the odd wedge that doesn't go with the set, or two woods of one set and one of another. That doesn't work for me. I try to concentrate on having all the clubs of the same weight and the same feel, all set up from the same manufacturer. That seems to make sense.

Sometimes, when you stand to a ball, the caddie can give you the wrong club. Once I asked for a nine-iron and he gave me a six. The ball was still climbing when it cleared the houses, never mind the green, because it was too much club. More recently it happened in reverse – I asked for a six and he gave me a nine – but I knew it was wrong the moment I got hold of it. You must get used to the feel. I don't think I could adapt to a strange wedge, iron or whatever. For me they all have to slot in and all have the same 'feel'.

Golfers love gimmicks, but they are divided over the long-stemmed putter used by the likes of Sam Torrance. I have had a go at one and I must confess I can see the point, because putting is the only part of the game where the right hand takes over. Assuming you are a right-handed golfer, the left hand is the prime mover in playing all the shots, except in the case of the putter when the right hand tries to 'bowl' the ball along the green into the hole. It is a stroke and not a hit. A big putter makes sense because it is an obvious pendulum – but it looks unwieldy to me.

I do see that being so long it is easier to keep it straight. With a normal-sized putter sweeping from right to left through the ball there is a tendency to push or pull or cut it. But then again the long putters look and feel like the long rest at snooker, and I was never happy with that. My uncle Tom, who was good at snooker, used to refer to the long rest as 'the furniture' – 'Don't get the furniture out, son – forget it. I'd rather hit something else!' The long putter may be effective for Torrance but I couldn't be bothered.

NELLIE THE ELEPHANT
THE SWING DOCTOR

The trouble is you look such a twit at our level, staggering on the green with one of them and then missing the putt. It looks good when Torrance does it, but out there on the midden – forget it!

I'm beginning to believe that the best way to putt is to copy my pal Stan, a stalwart golfer from way back, and the scourge of Bootle golf course.

Stan's motto is very simple: 'Assume all putts are dead straight and hit them at 100 mph – don't give them a chance to borrow.' Honestly, the number of his putts I've seen hit the back of the cup, fly a foot in the air and drop in. It's very spectacular but no good for the nerves when he's your partner. 'It's only a game, son,' he would say. 'Only a game …'

I love the nicknames that golf can produce. We have a guy, nameless for my own safety, who is called the Quizmaster. He keeps coming into the clubhouse saying, 'I've found the answer!' Well, he might think he has – until the next round!

I'll never forget the best lesson I ever had. David Lloyd is the pro at the West Lancs Club, a smashing bloke and one of my favourite teachers. He and Doug Currey, alias 'The Swing Doctor', from Filey have between them given me some semblance of a golf game. Neither of them is overawed by fame or fortune and can gently 'bully' you into good habits.

David had me practising shots with the feet together, feeling the rhythm and gently learning how to 'groove in' the swing, controlling the right shoulder, careful not to lurch into the ball, holding it all back till the crucial moment.

If only he'd been six months earlier with this particular lesson he could have saved me a lot of pain. I was appearing in Blackpool and arranged a Saturday morning knock with two pals I hadn't seen since schooldays.

On the first I felt generous, giving them shots all round. Then I saw them tee off well and the devil inside was already saying, 'Wow! Never mind a steady start with a four-wood. You'll have to go for the big one!'

So it was the driver with no warm-up. A mighty heave and I hit the ball a good way but immediately felt a stabbing pain in my chest.

'Heart attack!' I panicked but no, thank God. It was only a pulled muscle in the diaphragm area, making it impossible to play even a second shot. 'Goodbye lads,' I said, 'see you in the bar!' The next thing I was being looked after by a football club physio in the clubhouse. 'Tell you what you've tried to do – knock the skin off it while your muscles were still cold. I bet it hurts!' He didn't have to tell me that.

Meantime what were my pals thinking? 'We haven't seen that O'Connor for 18 years … funny bloke. Shortest round I've ever seen anyone play. Mind you he always was a nutter at school …'

Ever had that desire to read people's minds and discover the real thoughts behind their outward reactions? Take the Wang Open, a Pro-Celebrity-Am tournament, and on the tee is Ian Woosnam, accompanied by my wife's hero, 'Wobbly' the caddie (these Yorkshire folk stick together, you know!)

Woosie hit a ball to the limit of my vision and Wobbly said 'Rubbish. Topped it!'

I paced out that drive – it was at least 280 yards. Were they just having me on?

FIFTEENTH HOLE

It Works For Me!

PEOPLE ASK ME, though not very often, what is the secret of my golfing success? I would not presume to set myself up as a good teacher of the game – I'm no Jacobs or Leadbetter – but I can tell you what works for me, what I have discovered through my own follies and foibles. You never know, you may discover it's simply a piece of cake! Read on …

No matter how good a swing you have, and no matter how good an eye for the ball, if your basic set-up isn't correct, you are not going to strike the ball properly. You will hit the ball, but its direction will be governed by luck and not by skill.

The basic skill, therefore, is to align yourself properly. Try to think in terms of, say, two railway lines or two sides of the road. Standing on one railway line are your feet, and on the other, parallel to you of course, is the ball – and hence the back of the club. If that is not achieved immediately, no matter what else happens, the ball will not be struck correctly. If the lines diverge, the club-face will come in across the ball and knock it to a slice. If they converge, the result will be a hook. So the stance and the alignment are vital.

The grip is also very important. The best advice I ever

had came from Peter Alliss, who recommended me to hold my hands together as if to clap them, and then put a club between them. The only way the hands can then hold the club is the correct way. So remember – clap hands, here comes the club …

After the stance and the grip comes timing. It matters a lot how fast or how slowly you take away the club and how correctly you turn your whole body. Remember the lady who taught me to sing 'Nellie the Elephant' to myself – anything to help the tempo. The slower you can swing the better, because the most important part of any swing is the last six inches, just prior to hitting the ball, then striking the ball and then following it through.

You can swing as hard as you like over your head – it might look good but that doesn't count for anything. The most important speed of swing is right at the bottom of the pendulum. So if we think pendulum we grasp the fact that the only reason the club is going backward is to propel it forward. It's going back to be part of that smooth pendulum action.

Everything now should be a piece of cake; and in fact, it might help you to imagine you're standing vertically with your arms out at an angle to your body. The club is an extension of your arms and when the whole set-up swings it's like taking a slice out of that imaginary cake.

The swing isn't up and down: it's also around and across, a three-dimensional movement. It makes a plane at 45 degrees to your body. The speed at which you take away the club-face and, more importantly, the speed at which you return it will determine whereabouts the ball eventually lands. Because if the club-face is square, the only thing that can alter the ball going straight is if you bring it in too quickly and make it angle one way or the other. If you bring the club back slowly and return it along the same path every time, you should hit the ball straight – every time. The only things that change this are nerves, panic, anger, and all those other elements that have to be under control!

The only other way I can imagine the route a swing should take is to imagine a fat mayoress and think of the way her chain would lie across her chest.

Actually, one of the funniest sights is a man who has had a basic early lesson in golf and tries to do everything he has been told. We're back here to the 'nose to the grindstone, shoulder to the wheel' syndrome. Some look quite deformed as they swing because they are trying to improve on the pro's advice, carrying it to extremes.

When the pro says, 'You know why you're not getting the right result – it's because you're not standing near enough to the ball,' some folk over-compensate and actually stand on top of it. Instead of saying, 'I'll go forward a quarter of an inch and see if it helps,' some golfers think, 'If the remedy is getting near, let's see how near I can get. If I end up with the ball behind me I don't care …'

Don't exaggerate the pro's instructions. Instead, do whatever is comfortable for you, because at the end of the day there might be a thousand guys who look good when they swing but only a hundred of those who play well.

People say there is a correct way of doing things – but what is correct these days? If you look at Trevino's swing, it's not good according to the purist. Nancy Lopez was the best lady golfer in the world but her swing was all her own. No one tries to make you imitate Trevino or Lopez – but they all try to make you copy Faldo with his immaculate swing. Who's to say you can swing like him anyway and feel right doing it? If you have a couple of stone more round the waist you haven't a hope – so that's it. 'Correctness', then, is whatever feels comfortable for you and whatever gives you consistency.

We're back to the maxim, 'Whatever suits you …' If you can get on to a driving range or a practice ground,

You can't swing like Faldo, so that's it

develop a swing you are happy with and, say, eight times out of ten, hit the ball roughly in the direction and for the distance you want, then that's it. No need to improve on that because you aren't aiming to play in the Open anyhow. Alternatively, you could use the golf secretary's style – keep your head down and let the club do all the work!

As I said before, no one ever tells you how to drink a pint of lager. You just pick it up and drink it. But try to teach someone exactly how to do it – it's very difficult to explain – the way to grip the glass, the correct inclination of the arm, the right angle at the elbow, and at the last moment the split-second timing of when to open your mouth ... never mind how to drink a pint of lager on a ship that's pitching and rolling.

People can do it but they don't necessarily know how.

Apart from the basic shots taught by the pro, it is as well to have other shots in your locker, either worked out by yourself or copied from others. For instance, I watched Tom Kite at the American Open play a particular shot brilliantly. It's one I have mastered only because I play with old men – a pitch and run shot – which the guys I play with call a 'scuttery' shot. Trevino calls it a 'bump and run' shot.

Basically it's a stab with a seven- or eight-iron from about 40 yards off the green. You need to know how to play it because one of the hardest shots in golf, particularly if the wind is blowing, is a short one. A pro playing a 320-yard par four could, in theory, very nearly drive the green. But he wouldn't. He would play an iron short of the green and leave himself a full shot – a full sand wedge or a full wedge shot to throw the ball up and stop it on the green, near the hole.

You or I would get out the wood, hit the ball as hard as we could to get as near as possible, and be left with something like 60 yards – which is a really awkward shot. On a summer's day it's hard to gauge how far 60 yards is and stop the ball. I would rather have 100 yards to go and hit it as hard as I could with a wedge, knowing it would not go much further past the flag, because that's roughly my distance with a wedge. A pro would try to leave himself a full shot with any club.

What we amateurs tend to do, because we want to hit the first as hard as we can, is to leave ourselves a shot so near the green that we find ourselves playing a short second shot we're not used to. So we try to play 40-50 yards, throwing the ball up in the air, and hopefully stopping it dead somewhere near the hole. If the wind's blowing, the ball is going to go anywhere. When Tom Kite was playing at Pebble Beach, that's what was happening. The hole was less than 150 yards. But because the wind was so strong, players were hitting everything into the rough, even into the sea.

The 'scuttery' shot, as played by the old boys, particularly up north, stabs the ball a mere three or four feet in the air. Then it bounces its way on to the green. It's a bit six of one, half a dozen of the other as to where it'll stop; but at least if you pitch it up into the air and let it bounce along it has some chance of staying on the green. If you throw it higher in the air and the wind gets it, it could go anywhere. This one is unaffected by the wind because it keeps nice and low. And there is truly an art to it: if you play these old guys you will find when they are 50 yards out from the green, they are deadly. They are down in two with one of these little 'scuttery' chips; a pitch and run, and a putt and they're down.

Every golfer has a shot that he can play that may be new to everyone else! Think about it. I was once about 120 yards from the green and under a tree. I couldn't play any kind of ordinary shot. 'What are you going to do?' smiled my partner, thinking he 'had' me. I showed him with my trusty five-wood!

Normally with a five-wood, if I hit it well, the ball goes about 220 yards – twice as much club as I need. But a five-wood has a flat face and I can actually play it from beneath a tree very low because it doesn't need to be lifted up but swung around. With an iron you have to stand up to hit the ball, but you can play a wood, because it has plenty of face, by standing back and sweeping lower. To be truthful, it is hardly my secret weapon – I learnt it from Ozzleball when we were playing in the Benson & Hedges.

The other shot I play is again from beneath low-lying foliage. Trevino told me that if I was under a tree and had to keep the ball down for a long way, I should play a six-iron off the back foot. It hits the ball not more than about a foot and a half off the ground, and it stays at that height. Same principle as the bump and run shot.

The unfortunate thing is that golfers of our ilk, unlike pros, need those shots simply to get us out of trouble!

Length of shot depends on strength and conditioning. For instance, John Jacobs's maxim, that there is a club in your bag for every shot – is true. A pro may take a six-iron to get to the green and you may take a three – but if you are both on the green, at the end of the day that's what it's all about. Golf is not a matter of how but how many. If you've taken four shots to the green and so has Sevvy Ballesteros, then who's to say he's any better than you are? (Well, probably everyone but you!)

I played in the Dunhill Masters with that marvellous South African player, Mark McNulty. Mark, unfortunately, was having a bit of a back problem, which is normal for golfers, even good golfers. He told me, 'Golf is one of those games where the more you think you know about it the more intricate it becomes.' I suppose that's right; it's all down to our concept of the game. When you're hitting the ball well it can be the easiest game in the world. The irony is that when you've played a bad shot you know at least three reasons why you've played it. When you've played a good shot, you've no idea why it was a good one and what you did differently.

If you could harness or bottle the technique and the tempo when you've played a good shot, you'd have a world best-seller. It's one of those things: we play golf at our level not expecting to play the perfect shot, so when it comes we are not ready for it. Everything goes together – the hands, the wrists, the arms, the shoulder, the feet – everything is in perfect unison. Then for the rest of that day and maybe for the next week we are still trying to re-enact that exact move. It's to do, again, with our frame of mind.

Sevvy reckons he has about 20 different things he could try when he's playing badly, different techniques he can apply to put his game back together – all of them aimed at steadying the brain, and preventing him from panicking. Yet many pros I've met can't explain why they play well one day and not another; and that is encouraging to the honest hacker like you and me.

But then, isn't that always the way? I think it was George Gershwin who, when asked, 'How do you write a musical?', replied, 'I can't tell you.' The questioner pointed out, 'But you wrote one when you were seven …' and he answered, 'Yes, but I didn't have to ask anybody how.'

Blessed are they who are naturally gifted at golf, those who can pick up a club, let fly and never have to worry about whether the line was inside or outside the lie of the ball or whether the swing was too hard or too soft. Blessed are they who can swing a club and hit it like the old codgers you see playing golf – the 70- and 80-year-olds who can still make a perfect swing, don't try to knock the ball out of the screws of the club and thoroughly enjoy their day.

It wasn't until my company decided to come up with a TV game based on golf that we realised the advances that have been made, even since I started to play. Our basic idea was to film contestants and their celebrity partners actually playing a hole, like the ninth at Carnoustie or the fourth at Turnberry or the second at Wentworth or whatever. When we approached a TV company with the idea, they said, 'That's fine. We can do all that in the studio.'

Of course they can – the whole thing can be re-enacted on a video screen. You stand on a teeing-off mat which is scanned by an infra-red sensor. Depending on how you hit the ball, the sensor can tell you how far it will go, and whether it will hook or slice. The shot is then transferred to the major screen which tells you your position relative to the bunker, the fairway or the rough. Thanks to modern technology, which is there to help you eliminate any possible wrong shots, bad swings, and so on, you can now learn golf without even setting foot on a golf course!

The aids to the game that are around nowadays are unbelievable. Video screens can show you exactly how your swing will look and compute the plane, and you can see it all explained in graphic detail. All this points to a new generation of potential players who should be able to do nothing else except play perfect golf!

The only things we are not catering for here are the brain and the good old British weather. In 10 or 15 years' time we shall see exactly what these video tutors have passed on to the youngsters, and how they cope with the elements.

I guess I was lucky to live for a long while in an area which has to be the perfect breeding ground for golfers in all conditions: the north-west coast with its string of good links courses, like Royal Birkdale, Hillside (probably one of the most difficult courses), plus a club where I'd be delighted to be a member – West Lancashire. That really is a different course if the wind is blowing. It can blow there for a long time and very strongly. Add that to the mix of brain power, arms, hands, wrists, ankles, club-face square to the ball, tempo of swing. As the ball leaves the club at whatever speed, it is hit by a 70 mph gale coming from left or right (or I swear in some cases, both ways at once!). And when the ball lands it can hit anything – a dry patch, a wet patch, a brick, somebody's foot, a watering nozzle on the edge of the green – and end up anywhere.

There are wonderful stories of balls doing the most amazing things. There was one ball that was lost and eventually found in the hood of somebody's anorak. Or you could hit a tree and the ball could ricochet anywhere. Generally, when the pros smack one into the trees it goes for good. With us amateurs, it usually just drops down, perhaps with a lucky bounce and within range – but who knows? All these elements have to be put into the pot before you can say, 'I've really got a grip of golf, I understand it all now – I've got it sussed!' And no video tutor is going to help you solve all the riddles and enigmas. For, when 99 per cent of things are going right for you, the shot can still be wrong. That's the astonishing thing.

Probably the greatest feeling in the game, other than hitting a perfectly fine shot, is to be able to stand on a tee and call one. When you announce, 'I'm going to hit this with a six-iron and I'm going to fade it around the corner and it should land by that white marker over there,' and then actually land the ball within a couple of feet of it, the sense of achievement is total.

Such things, however, are easier said than done. I once read about two golfers, Neil Coles and Brian Barnes, I believe, who were asked to play a round of 70-plus, and to state honestly how many shots (excluding putts) went exactly where they intended. They came up with only four or so occasions when they could truly say the ball landed in the spot where they would have run up and dropped it, given half the chance.

One of my favourite golfing songs is called 'Straight Down the Middle'. It was written by Sammy Cahn and Jimmy van Heusen especially for Bing Crosby and he is one of only two people I have ever heard sing it well. The other was the late and great Dickie Henderson – and it is significant that both these fine entertainers gave their all for the game of golf.

It truly has such lovely lines in it … '*I aimed it at two but it bounced off nine. The caddie said "Wait – because if you're still in the State, it's OK!"*' (What a wonderfully optimistic point of view.)

Then it goes: '*The life of a golfer is not all gloom, there's always the lies in the locker room …*' and that's so true. No matter how well or how badly you've played, who can stop you talking a good game?

Golf is probably one of the few games you can talk about informatively without actually being able to perform. I have seen fellers duff shots all over the course and then go in and complain about the conditions – the wind and the greens weren't holding, and so on – and they could be right. There are good golfers sitting there agreeing with them. Who's to know these moaners didn't even get to the greens?

I sometimes used that as my opening gambit at after dinner speeches: 'I'd like to thank the ground staff for the condition of the bunkers. I'd like to thank them for the greens as well, but sadly I didn't get near enough to one to form an opinion.'

SIXTEENTH HOLE

The Shot That Got Away

THE SOCIAL SIDE of golf is a marvellous thing. I suppose when one gets to the end of one's career, when one is 70-plus, it's probably a good three-quarters of what the game is all about anyway. And we'll always be able to talk about the shot that did the business or the one that only just got away.

I have never had a hole in one but I always maintain that a very close hole in two is always better-looking than a fluke hole in one. It's the ball that stops dead about three inches from the pin, and gets your playing partners saying, 'God, isn't he good – see how near he put that!' It's the old adage of being a near hit rather than a near miss. I know which one I would call the better shot.

In every golfer's memory, and consequently in his armoury, there will always be The Story – the one where he hit the flag and it dropped down and nearly went in the hole, the two that would have been a one and broken the course record. Not to mention the one that would have been the longest drive on the day but unfortunately rolled into the rough and wasn't counted.

So golf is a game of 'if onlys', marvellous memories and indisputable facts. Unless someone has gone all the way

You saw that didn't you, Lord?

round the course with you, how can they gainsay anything you claim?

There's the old tale of the guy who came into the clubhouse and said, 'You know that lake by the fifth – must be 300 yards or more from the tee. I hit a shot this morning that cleared the water and landed the ball in line with the pin. Great eagle shot – must have been all of 350 yards!' And one of his mates observed, 'Funny you should say that. I hit a ball down by the lake yesterday and do you know what I found – a lantern from an old Spanish galleon! And do you know the amazing thing – it was still alight!'

So his friend looked at him and said, 'I don't believe you ...' and he replied, 'I'll tell you what. You knock 80 yards off your shot and I'll blow out my lantern ...'

Then there was the sad tale about the parish priest who played a round of golf alone on a Sunday morning, sank a hole in one and had to keep it to himself. He stood there thinking, 'Who can I tell about this? I'm not supposed to be here in the first place!'

Probably the most enjoyable golf I ever played and a round I'm hoping to re-achieve sometime, was when I did a summer season in Scarborough. I had the whole health kick going – I gave up smoking, gave up drinking and tried to go on a strict diet all at the same time. It's amazing how much of a martyr that can make you feel. Every day is a minor triumph – no cigarette for so many hours, two pounds lost in a day, and so on. I also went into light training and used to jog a couple of miles before going on to the practice ground and hitting a bucket of balls, then went out to play the course. Surprisingly, that was the most consistently good golf I've ever played.

I suppose that's understandable because if the brain's sharp from the running and the fresh air, then the rest of the system is alert and warmed up before you start. If I had to give pointers to would-be successful golfers I would say be a 'rested' golfer. Don't play when you're tired because you have to get your head together and concentrate. And don't ever take a mobile phone with you on a course – that is the kiss of death.

Be as loose as possible, do as much warming up as possible. Try not to play a serious game the day after a lesson. Remember the old gag: 'I couldn't play that well, I was seriously injured – I had a lesson yesterday.' Lessons are marvellous if you want to get your game right, but don't expect to play a match the next day for a fiver and still try to do all the things the pro told you, because when things start to go wrong you will return to your old habits and have wasted a lesson. You will have lost the game, and the fiver as well. Always keep a good perspective on your health and the game, and give any lesson time to sink in, time for you to practise it yourself before attempting to emulate it.

Fitness is essential, but not the ultimate. If fitness were everything, you wouldn't have any chubby golfers or chubby snooker players, would you?

The eye is a wonderful machine – so get your eye in! It will correct things for you. While the stance is very important, the eye will try to make you do what it can see. If the eye sees the shot as being straight, it will make you play straight, no matter what. If you are going to play at that tree, the eye knows where the tree is even though you're not facing it and will make you pull away from the trouble, almost without your realising it.

The phrase 'Out of the corner of the eye' should be allied with the bad back syndrome. You are about to do one thing and the eye corrects your action subconsciously! Perhaps you spot an overhanging branch out of the corner of your eye. Even though it's only a twig, it can seem enormous and it can put you off – sometimes you have to overrule your eye – but it's hard, because you always know it's there.

If you think you're going to hit the tree, you are drawn to it. The head is saying, 'Go over there where it's safe' … and it's true. The eye will try to over-compensate for any trouble and you can't kid it. It says to the brain, 'The tree is over there – hit this way.' It's like the story of the vicar with the big nose. Everyone tried to ignore the fact except one old lady who said, 'Have a cup of tea, vicar. How many sugars would you like in your nose?'

A retired old pro once said to me, 'If you have swung correctly, when the head comes up your eye should follow the direction in which the ball has gone.' This is true because basically you are keeping your head down until the club has hit the ball and then the whole thing follows on … You can't kid the eye, therefore you have to gear everything else up so that when you hit the ball it goes where the eye wants it to go.

It is very difficult on a wet day to play in glasses. I now play in contact lenses – I'm fortunate in that my eyes are equally shortsighted, so I can put one lens in for driving, and leave the other eye for putting. I've tried the other way – wearing the glasses for putting and taking them off for driving, but it doesn't work. So I drive with my right eye and putt with my left. I guess a cross-eyed golfer will always put it in the bunker: They said, 'Follow the ball with your eye,' and he said, 'It could have gone anywhere …'

When you are in trouble, out scouting in Apache country, it really is your own fault if you haven't read the guide book. We should absorb all the things that can help us. At least read the rules on the back of the card; more often than not they will give you a clue as to how to get out of a fix. Rabbit scrapings, ground under repair, various lies in various places, where you can move your ball without penalty – the rules are there to help you avoid trouble. It's no use saying the pros have all the advantages because they know all the rules; you should too. And the local rules as well – those adjustments that only apply to that particular course.

If your ball is in trouble, the first thing to do is get it safe. There's no point thinking, 'If I were to whack this and kept it a foot off the ground and drill it hard, just slightly right of that tree, it might get on the green.' That's a mighty big 'if' – if we could all play that shot we wouldn't be carrying our own bags. We'd all have a caddie and be playing in the Open.

Obviously you have to get the ball back on the fairway. And don't panic! If it's a par four and you're in the bushes off the tee, you could still be on the green in three and with a bit of luck be down in four, or take a five (if your partner is giving you a shot this hole so much the better). So swallow your pride, accept that luck evens itself out in the end, make the best of it, and get back to where you can play properly.

Assume that now and again in your golfing life you are going to land in a bunker. It really pays to practise getting out of bunkers. The keen golfer should start at the practice ground, hit 20 or 30 balls, continue on to the putting green or the chipping green, and then go into the practice bunker. If possible, spend five minutes in the bunker to get the feel of it. For a start, it matters what kind of sand is in there, whether it's wet or dry, thin or heavy. In some bunkers the sand is like sugar, in others it's like plasticine.

At Ascot I have known five different consistencies of sand in the bunkers! And you don't know until you are in, what you are up against. So don't forget to practise bunker shots – and try to assess how, if need be, you can get out within the rules. There are certain things you can't do and which you have to adjust to when playing out of a bunker. You can't ground your club, for instance, before you hit the ball; but you can walk in and just from

'LOVELY AND COMFY
I'LL TAKE 'EM'
56
WAIST
24
LEG

your footfall and the feel of the sand you should gain some idea of what kind of trouble you are in. And depending on how you are lying depends on how you are going to play the shot – whether you will take a lot of sand or no sand or flick it off the top.

Wear comfortable clothes on the golf course, too. Don't buy a brand new pair of shoes and expect to play perfect golf in them first time out. If they pinch or rub, they are going to ruin your concentration, as will a sweater that is tight under the arms or whatever. No matter that your sweet Aunt Lily knitted it for you – wear what you feel comfy in.

I wear 32/31 (32 waist, 31 inside leg) but sometimes I see in golf shops trousers marked up at 56/24. I'd love to meet him – Cinderella in reverse! It doesn't matter how abnormal that guy looks, if he feels right that's all that matters.

Mia Carla, a bonny girl who could be mistaken for a Roly Poly, is a great comedienne and a good singer as well. She has taken up golf and her biggest worry is how to swing a club around her chest – is it over or under?

A lady who is well endowed has to make this decision very early in her career, because it will determine whether she uses irons or woods. Mia has now sorted herself out with woods, which means she is swinging around herself – and that's fine. It works for her.

The saddest sight is the guy who, for one reason or another, usually for health, has been told by his doctor to diet and lose something like six stone. He has been conditioned all his life to swinging round this girth, this lump of lard in front of him. Now he finds he is swinging more upright and has to learn tempo all over again. With the weight gone, he virtually has to rejig his whole game to hit the ball as well as he did before.

You have to customise what you use to the way you play and the way you look.

SEVENTEENTH HOLE

Celebs and Showbiz Partners

BERNARD DELFONT once maintained we would never have had an American top of the bill in Britain if it hadn't been for our golf courses, and it's probably true. The likes of Bing Crosby and Bob Hope were lured over here by the prospect of playing golf – entertaining was probably a secondary consideration!

Don't forget it was in 1952 at Maidenhead that Bing and Bob Hope played the first ever showbiz celebrity challenge golf match in the British Isles; they challenged Ted Ray and Donald Peers. And so great was the crowd, it swamped the course so that the game had to be abandoned. There are wonderful pictures of Bing and Bob riding across this golf course in an open car being pursued by fans with the other two players clinging to the running boards.

There is an apocryphal story about The Ink Spots, too, in their early days. Val Parnell and Bernard Delfont had both agreed on the maximum sum they could pay the group to work their respective venues – the Palladium and the Prince of Wales. Instead of outbidding each other to put them on, they played a game of golf to decide who would get them. So golf is very important to showbiz.

One of the best celebrity golfers, a man who in his time

I believe played off scratch, is Christopher Lee. But then nobody is likely to mess with Christopher Lee!

Jimmy Tarbuck is a marvellous golfer with a handicap of five. He may not always win competitions but he will always be within a point or two of his handicap, and will always deliver the goods, which is pretty good going. I played with him once on a course he had never played, on a funny old day weather-wise, and he was a bit shattered. Yet he still came within a few points of his handicap, leaving me for dead!

Roy Walker is also a very low handicap golfer. Roy used to be a left-handed shot-putter but he plays golf with his right hand. If he is innately strong in his left arm, then he is certainly going to have an advantage over the rest of us – and he uses his strength well.

The best celebrity striker of a golf ball was Val Doonican. I think he was off two at the time and he is a very fine player. But then you'd expect him to be on song. When a pro hits the ball it climbs and keeps on climbing even when it's falling. Doonican was the only celeb I ever saw do that – send his ball off the tee like a rocket and knock it a mile.

Of the fun-type golfers, Norman Collier is a lot of fun; and no matter what time of the day it is you'll know where Frank Carson is on a course because you can hear him – unless he's doing well. If he's building a good score he'll be silent. He's a grand Irishman, and wasn't it an Irish golf pro who actually said these marvellous words on a very wet day: 'D'you know, if it wasn't my job I wouldn't do this for money, even if you paid me!'

I won't say it's the worst swing in the world, but Stan Boardman's swing is certainly unique! I couldn't describe it but I'd advise people to go and see it in action. I know some golfers who have heard about it and travel for miles to see him swing. Yet the amazing thing is … it works. When he takes a practice swing, observers remark, 'Now that's funny!' Then he hits the ball the same way and they all do a double take. 'Now wait a minute ... did he really do that?' He's got a good eye for the ball though, has Stan – he used to be a footballer.

Bruce Forsyth is a good steady golfer and like Tarby, he will always deliver the goods. Little Ronnie Corbett, who uses specially shortened clubs, is proof that you don't have to be massive to hit the ball a long way, because he has timing and rhythm. The art in his case, being a small man, is to get everything he's got behind the ball – and he does it so well.

I have played quite a lot of golf with Russ Abbot, who's a good golfer – I think he's a twelve now, and he takes his golf very seriously. What I like about Russ is that he's a stickler for the etiquette of golf – very precise and dignified. Precision is the secret of his successful career and with his wonderful gift of inventing characters. He doesn't have to wait for whoever is next going to be popular on telly – he has a wealth of comic characters in his head.

Shakin' Stevens too is a consistent golfer – though he does tend to shake his knees even when he putts! He is a nice player and excellent company.

Of the ladies, Rachel Heyhoe Flint plays off eight and is a good steady player, a natural sportswoman. Another fine striker of the ball is the actress Suzanne Danielle, who is married to Sam Torrance.

Lee Trevino reckons the best swing he has ever seen on a lady is Mary Parkinson. He says she is one of the few golfers whose practice swing is the same as her ordinary swing. Most people swing nice and steady in practice and then give it loads in their actual swing. But Mary gives them both the same treatment, which is ideal and what we all aim for. She is a lovely player. Parky's not bad either.

You would expect guys who play other sports to take to

golf naturally. Nigel Mansell, Ian Botham, Fred Trueman, Richie Benaud and Ted Dexter for example, are all good players. For cricketers especially, golf is marvellous for keeping fit and enjoying later in life. They don't need to run at 100 mph and limber up. It's a good game for them to play and they can adjust accordingly.

Among many soccer players – Kenny Dalglish is a fine golfer. And I admire Alan Hansen, the Scots international. He is a very low golf handicapper, played rugby for Scotland as well as soccer and basketball. And he's a good-looking feller and a talker. Dammit!

One of the most amazing guys at golf is Brian Close – because he can play left or right-handed and has two different handicaps. It's true! He is very low handicap, if not scratch, with one hand and four or five with the other. So it would be impossible to get him into trouble because there are shots where a right-hander would be stuck against a wall or a tree and he could play out left-handed! Maybe he keeps one or two left-handed clubs in his bag just in case. Not many can do that trick. Bernhard Langer, I believe, played one such amazing shot out of a tree with his wrong hand. If you only have a right-handed club you can end up performing some contortions on the course, where a left-handed club could help!

I always have a straight-faced putter in my bag – straight-faced on both sides – and I can use that when up against a wrong 'un. I am not saying other putters are no good, but for safety, I always have a straight-faced one.

A number of sterling characters form the backbone of the Variety Club's Golf Society and the Comedians' Golf Society as well as the Stage Golf Society. These clubs consist of people in the entertainment world who love the game of golf, and in one way or another, throughout the year, help to raise funds for many worthwhile charities or projects, like the Variety Club's Sunshine Coaches.

I could namedrop a whole roll call – Roger de Courcy, Henry Cooper, Henry Kelly, Mike Reid and so on – as well as those already mentioned, who are willing to travel hundreds of miles at their own expense. They not only travel and play all day, but also do a little entertainment in the evening, all for the good of golf and in the name of charity.

Ask me who are the pros I love to watch, and Trevino has to be the man, because he has a gag for every hole; he's the funniest guy and he is the most all-round professional. He would have been a success at anything – even a very good stand-up comedian had he put his mind to it. Or in any other sport too, he would have excelled because he has such a good eye and such fine coordination. What with his sharp wit, plus being a top-class golfer, he is a terrific ambassador for the game.

Golfers are special people. Without exception they are probably the greatest sportsmen in the world, followed (with minor exceptions!) by snooker players. Golfers have enormous patience, too – even more so than cricketers. You may be 22 behind on the first day of a golf tournament, but you carry on because by the fourth day you could be back in the frame. It's a matter of waiting for your chance and taking that chance – not throwing your clubs on the floor and giving up in digust.

Trevino I could watch all day – but it's difficult to say who isn't a hero. I like Woosnam as a man and he is great when he is on form: he can knock a ball a mile. Sevvy is the people's favourite, good-looking and capable of playing shots that others wouldn't dare take on.

Sandy Lyle is coming back now. I have a feeling Sandy will be all right if he doesn't get too much advice! It's very easy for everyone to tell you what you are doing wrong and what you should do to put it right. Sandy is young enough to learn life's greatest lesson – you need to be down to be up.

To be a successful comic you have to die on your feet. The only way you're going to get better is to go in there and be shown that you ain't the business, that there's more to it than you. And if there's a salutary lesson to be had, then I reckon Sandy's had it. The deeper the trough has gone, the more strength you gain when the next high comes. I have a lot of confidence in Sandy – we'll hear a lot more of him, maybe more than we heard before. I have played with him when he was on song and the ball used to scream when it left the club. He could pinpoint shots – say, 'I'm going to put it there' – and he did.

It's like a snooker player, on a smaller field of course, saying, 'I'm going to hit the blue and leave the white nestling behind the pink – for all you watching in black and white.' But when a guy can do that from 300 yards, it's really impressive.

Jacklin was the best hitter of the ball I've ever heard, the cleanest, sweetest hitter … in his time so I'm told, was Alliss, but I never saw or heard him. But when Jacklin hit the ball you knew it was hit.

I like watching lady pros because they are so graceful – the only man who comes close is Hale Irwin. At his peak he was the most graceful swinger. He didn't look as if he'd hit it very far but he was proof that if it looks good it must be good. If a golf swing finishes nicely then the ball must finish nicely as well. He sacrificed power for this grace and artistry, and he guided the ball more than he smashed it.

Nicklaus was graceful and natural and that's why he stayed at the top so long. I heard that as he got older he had to learn how to chip a ball – because he'd never had to do it before. He had to learn the 60-yard pitch and run – he'd never needed it before because he was so powerful. Then, as his power waned, he introduced new shots into his locker. The story goes that it was his son who taught him how to play one shot when he started finding himself

40 yards short of a target he would have hit at his peak. 'Come here dad – let me show you ...' Can you imagine that!

One of the last rounds of golf Henry Cotton played, bless him, was at Ascot. I sadly missed him, but I was told he could still hit the ball and was a hard man to beat even in old age. That's why it's such a good game – the only one where a pro can give you a start and still play you. McEnroe might give you three points every game – 40 love down and still win. Steve Davis could give you a 50-point start at snooker and batter you. But Trevino or Sevvy could give me a regulation handicap start – say seven shots – and with a fair wind and good putting I could have a darn good try at holding them. At the end of the day it's still a game we can all play and all enjoy without getting slaughtered.

Golf has always had a Brit in the top ten. The same applies to motor racing, of course, but that's not quite in the same league. As for summer sports, we can't do it in tennis, our cricket comes and goes – yet in golf we have Faldo, Woosnam, Lyle and many more capable of winning major tournaments. Why? Is it the range of courses available in Britain, or our temperament, our weather, our innate love of the game?

The short answer to all these questions has to be 'Yes'. Certainly the Americans love playing over here. I think it's marvellous when Americans can adapt to our game. We enthuse when we win something in America, but when we go out and play in their conditions, the weather is generally a lot better, and the greens are slicker. The Yanks who come over here have a lot more to contend with – they end up almost playing in snow, often in howling rain and gales – and all credit to them.

We have so many different kinds of courses, and one thing you can't beat is healthy competition. In boxing,

Frank Bruno can practise and spar for hundreds of rounds, but it's not like fighting a challenger over ten rounds. Competition is necessary. Generally there are enough golf competitions around for our pros to keep that edge, because you need that extra sharpness which you get when you don't play for fun. We have it, thankfully, in golfing terms. Wouldn't it be lovely if all the sports we played had that same competitive edge?

American courses, by and large, tend to be man-made and well manicured, whereas ours are mostly natural and range from the rugged Scottish courses to the lush greens of the south.

The greatest accolade I heard came from one of the record holders of the British Open, Tom Watson, who maintains that one of the best courses in the world is Dornoch in Scotland. That is his favourite all-time course. Now he has played everywhere and even built courses, and if he is willing to pick Dornoch as his number one, it has to be right.

We tend to take our great courses for granted – yet Americans make pilgrimages. I was up at Turnberry once with Tony Jacklin and Brian Huggett for a big Pro-Celebrity-Am day and the weather was appalling. The flags were almost horizontal, and it was blowing a gale. Gordon Banks was there, Freddie Trueman, Peter Parfitt – we all came in and said 'Forget it.' It was that bad. So we had a Question of Sport session in the hotel instead.

Yet four Yanks played the course that day. They said, 'We've come 5000 miles and we ain't missing this.' They came in like snowmen at the end, freezing yet totally exhilarated. But then that's dedication: they'd come miles and they were willing to suffer anything to realise their dream!

The Japanese are the same – they come to Wentworth, buy everything in sight and sometimes don't play! Just take everything home with them to prove they've been here.

We love the Americans, but don't forget they tend to talk differently to us! John Jacobs, apparently, when he went to America for the first time to do golf commentaries, didn't appreciate that Americans have different terminologies to ours. This guy had hit his ball out of the bunker and taken no sand, just flicked it off the top. Over here we would call that a 'pecker' (like chicken pecking corn), which of course has a totally different connotation in the States. So when John said, 'This man looks like a pecker,' they gave him some very odd looks. It all went very quiet in the box.

It was like the American GIs, when they came here during the war, and were told by the girls they met in the Forces canteens: 'Keep your pecker up!' – they thought to themselves: 'Boy, what a great country!'

Then John turned to his companion in the commentary box and confided, 'Can't wait for the commercial break. I'm dying for a fag.' That was his reputation gone up in smoke!

But we can get our own back if we want to. There's a story told of an American group in this country, over for a golfing tour and being treated after a day of golf and good company at a North Country club to a typical northern evening out – hot pot supper, red cabbage, the lot – no expense spared. There's even a waiter in what passes for an evening suit doing the rounds, giving out the pats of butter to accompany the rolls. And this American says to him, 'I'll have two of those, please.' The waiter says, 'Look mate. I've got orders. One plate, one pat of butter.' The American insists, 'But I always have two.' Again the waiter answers, 'Listen mate, I don't care what you always have. I've been told – one plate, one pat of butter.'

So the American asks, 'Do you know who I am?' The waiter says, 'No.' So the American tells him: 'I am a multimillionaire businessman in America, I have a business that goes into 48 states, I've got a 200,000-acre ranch. I've got five oil wells ...' And the waiter replies, 'Do you know who I am?' And the American says, 'No.' And the waiter says, 'I'm the bloke with the butter.'

EIGHTEENTH HOLE

Around With O'Connor

THE GREATEST moment of my golfing life came when I played in a Celeb-Am tournament at Patshull Park near Wolverhampton, arranged by Rachel Heyhoe Flint. Nicholas Parsons and Roger de Courcy were there; so was Bernie Cribbins. Par for the course was 71 and I parred it. That is the only time I have parred a proper course. I have gone round the back nine of an eighteen-hole course and parred that, but I actually parred Patshull.

It was a lovely summer's day and the putts all went down. I was playing off eight, so I was basically eight shots better than my handicap. Even so, our team got 94 points. We were playing in a four-ball and you picked the best two scores on each hole – and we got 94, which is massive. Theoretically, if we all played to handicap we should shoot 72. But with 94 we weren't even in the first three. No names will be mentioned – but Bernard Cribbins won it. He's a lovely man and he was mentioned in dispatches. I stood up at the dinner in the evening and said, 'I'd like to read you Bernard Cribbins's score card. It begins, "Once upon a time ..." '

The only way to learn better golf is to play with better people. Just like the only way to look young is to hang around with old folk. You may think you're at the top of your sphere, but it is only when you play in Pro-Celeb-Ams with the likes of Lyle or Trevino that you appreciate there is a totally different dimension to the game. The things you think are important mean nothing to them.

They say, 'Never mind where you were taught to place your feet, stand like this ...' It's like learning maths – you start with basic sums, adding up and taking away, dividing, multiplying. By the time you get to the sixth form, you are doing logarithms and calculus, and it all becomes one great experience; everything else is so elementary.

When you are playing with a pro who is saying, 'I am going to place the ball there because of this factor and that factor,' you worry about whether your toe is in line with your other foot. Suddenly it's a totally different ball game – and yet it isn't. You learn more about priorities playing with better players.

So here are some of the tips I have learnt from players better than I will ever be! The first rule I was ever given for teeing off – and it still works for me today – is look at the tee, look at where you're aiming to put the ball. On most holes you should be able to see the flag, unless it's a dog-leg or over a hill or whatever. Generally speaking, you can see the flag or where the flag ought to be. Look at where you want the ball to be for your second shot.

On certain holes, like a par five, there's a certain amount of forgiveness. You can actually stray quite a way out on a par five and put yourself back again, because you're going to take three shots to get to the green – if the first shot is wayward, the second can rectify it. But on a par four where, for regulation, you have to be on in two, your first shot is all-important.

Now there's going to be trouble on one side of the hole, maybe even on both sides, and you have to decide whereabouts your ball will be best placed. You don't want it to be in or near the trouble, either for this or your second shot. On a dog-leg hole, if it's a dog-leg to the left, ideally you want to be at the apex of the bend on the right at the end of shot one, looking up the rest of the fairway at the hole. The big hitter will try to go over the trees and land it short of the green, but it's a lot more risky for you. You want to have a clear shot at the flag for your second.

When you tee up you have to be aware of where the ball is going to go. I've always maintained – and it's worked for me every time – that you should play away from where you don't want to be! Sounds simple, but you'd be surprised how many rushes of blood to the head can occur out there on a golf course!

If you want to be on the right-hand side of the fairway, tee up on the left-hand side of the tee. And vice versa. This minimises the temptation of going over the trees and cutting the corner. The chances of you or I going over high trees is one in five – and that's praise. And if you do get over, you are only left with a shot that's too short for you to work out. It looks good for macho man if there is a group of female spectators he wants to impress, and who are going to coo, 'My God, can't he hit the ball!' But at the end of the day who cares? What counts is who's got the money. Drive for show, putt for dough!

You always tee up on the side where there's trouble; if it's on the left, tee up on the left and play away from it. Your eye will take you away from the trouble and your hands and your body will follow … it says here!

Secondly, you are thinking ahead and picking your second shot. All the pros play each hole backwards – they know what shots they are going to play to get them down in three on a par four. The best you can aim for is par, so do yourself a favour and think ahead. Leave yourself 100 yards for the second shot and work it out in your head. I've got 350 yards this hole … I need to hit 250 or so with a three-wood to that spot … then a nine-iron to the green. We should know within five yards how far we can hit each club – a seven-iron is 140 yards, a six-iron is 150 and so on. So we can work it back: to leave us a nice eight or nine to the green we need to take a three- or four-wood from the tee.

Also we have to be aware that the wind can play tricks: the easiest wind to play in is the one immediately behind you or the one right in your face. The hardest one is the one that's coming left or right, because goodness knows how strong it is. The trick there is to look up and see what the wind is doing to the treetops – it's no good looking at the distant flag drifting softly in the breeze. Look up into the trees and watch the branches swaying madly about – because up there is where the ball is going to go.

If you were going to pot the ball like a snooker shot, there would be no problem, because there would be no wind resistance along the ground. But if you are about to hit an eight-iron 60/70 feet in the air you need to know what's happening up there. Try to do this all in the few minutes you are setting your stall out and preparing to hit the ball – it is all-important.

The second shot, assuming you are in a good position, will be to the green, and now you have to pick whereabouts on the green you want to be. The men who lay out greens are very crafty. On an ordinary day the hole will be easy, sited somewhere in the middle; so you just aim at the flag, and whatever happens you're safe. On competition days they will put the flag behind a bunker, or as near to the edge of the green as regulations allow – which I think is six feet. This time you can aim at the flag and maybe go just a little too far and find yourself rolling off the green and maybe into a bunker. Or into the water.

So the rule for hackers is: no matter where the flag is, go for the middle of the green. At least then you are on the green. A maxim I learnt from Gary Player years ago

The hardest wind is the one coming from left or right

is always to play over the flag because all the trouble is usually to the front of the green. Certainly that used to be true but it isn't always so nowadays. People are beginning to put trouble at the back. There are places at the back of the greens now where Red Indians live!

Therefore we shouldn't really be wondering what side of the green we need to be on: we should be aiming for the middle.

Mind you, having said that about the trouble, have a look at where the bunkers are placed, because that will give you an idea of the lie of the hole. If the bunkers or the trees or the water are on the left, it must mean that the ground runs that way or the wind blows that way. There is usually a reason why they are sited there to grab your ball. And the maxim here is the same as for the fairway: play safe, protect your par to the centre of the green, and then it's between you and your putt.

Everything sounds simple when you hear it for the first time, and you wonder why you didn't think of it before! The best tip I ever learnt about putting was to imagine that the flag was really in the middle of a bucket. So when you are putting to the hole pretend you are actually aiming into a bucket about two feet in diameter. If you can get the ball into that diameter then with your next shot you are bound to sink it because from two feet you can't miss.

It's like the old gag of the feller baling out of the plane, isn't it? They told him, 'For the parachute you pull this first cord – and if that doesn't work you pull this second cord.' And the feller asked, 'What happens if the second one doesn't work?' And they said, 'By that time you'll be about ten feet off the ground – and you can jump ten feet, can't you?' So get the ball within the rim of that imaginary bucket. The principle sounds simple – and it is – but it's so often forgotten. People play from about 20 feet trying to hole the ball. An ace pro will sink a 22-foot putt, but if you and I get it, it's a bonus. We simply aim in that direction, hoping to get it near.

So no rush of blood on the putting – aim for the bucket. If it's inside the bucket, it's a good three, you've scored and earned yourself a birdie. If you don't and you're still inside the bucket, you're going to get a four, which can't be bad.

Peter Alliss always said that putting is probably the most important part of anyone's game and certainly the stroke that is played most often, yet we seldom have a lesson on it. People tell us how to putt, possibly show us how to grip and suggest various tips, but no one spends an hour watching you putt, or helping you to putt properly when you are hitting drives or sand wedges or whatever. It's a part of the game we could all spend a little more time working on.

Having said that, I must confess I have a putting machine at home, where the ball rolls in and is returned to you automatically for another go. Actually the cat spends more time playing with it than I do …

What wins matches at our level is not having to three-putt and always getting at least a three on a par three. The things that can ruin an amateur's card are bad par threes and lousy putts. And when you think about it, if you shoot an 85, and 25 of those are putts, you would have had a very good round. Two putts a hole (36) represents over a third of your shots – so putting is very important.

Playing par threes well boils down to knowing what you can do well yourself. It's the Liverpool FC principle. The essence of their success is that they know what they can't do, so they don't do it! Remember that apocryphal quote of Bill Shankly, probably the best football manager of his time: 'Football isn't life or death – it's more important than that!'

It summed up Liverpool's dedication, and it is true with the Liverpool team that they don't play a specific game of football because it looks good. They have a system and it works really well. In fact it goes right through their organisation. They must be the only team in the world who can sign a goalkeeper for a million quid and put him in the reserves! Can't be bad.

The same is true about golf. My son Stephen is a powerful hitter of the ball. He is a big lad, one of the ilk – and there are a lot of them around in golf – who want to hit the ball a long way every time. So when I hit a five-iron he wants to hit a seven to show that he can hit a seven as far as I can hit a five. At the end of the day John Jacobs says, 'In every bag of clubs there is only one you have to hit as hard as you like and that's the driver. Everything else you can taper back.'

If Sevvy hits a four-iron 220 yards, I've got a four-wood that can do the same job. I don't have to use the same club as he does. As long as I have a club that will do the job, who cares? I don't have to be macho about it. At the end of the day if he gets a four and I get a four it doesn't matter that we did it using different techniques – even if I've hit a tree or someone on the head and the ball has rebounded and gone down the hole.

Yet there are people who psyche themselves out. Stephen used to be one of them, although he's mellowed now. When he took golf seriously, he had a massive driver – you have to be Rambo to pick it up let alone swing it – and he would hit it miles. But he would then rely on my judgement for the next shot. I would say I was going to use a five-iron – he would use a seven. In the end I stopped telling him what I was using. That made it difficult – now he had to guess which club I had taken out the bag.

So while I was hitting my shot, he would be looking in my bag. I sorted him out by getting head covers for all the irons – and putting them on the wrong clubs. He would see me take a club out with a seven-iron cover on it (it was really a five), pick a nine from his own bag and find he was nowhere near me – maybe 20 yards or more short.

And he couldn't fathom it for a long time.

But that was only because he wanted to play the game better than me. Instead of saying, 'This is my game and this is what I'm going to play,' he did what you see so many players doing. They'll stand on the tee and one will say to the other, 'What have you got there?' and the other says, 'A three-wood.' The first player then draws in his breath and says, 'I don't know so much ...' and he's psyching his opponent out now. The basic rule of golf is once you've taken a club out of your bag – hit it! That's the end of it. Even if it goes up in the air or it goes too far or too short – hit the ball well.

Buy a yardage chart – some clubs even give you the yardage on their score-cards now. And play the game to suit yourself. We can't all hit a ball 300 yards or we'd all be on the circuit. We can't all sing 'Delilah' or we'd all be getting Tom Jones's money. So we play it the best way we can.

NINETEENTH HOLE

Golfers' Heaven

EVERY GOLFER at one time or another has got to dreaming what it would be like in Golfers' Heaven. Over a relaxing drink or two at the bar after an exhausting round, they'll map out their ideal round on their ideal course.

No wind, no rain, no bunkers, no tees, always on the green in regulation, every putt a birdie, no holes in one because a hole in one always looks a fluke, but lots of nice holes in two – the first shot always inside the bucket, of course!

There would be no queueing on the tee; you'd always tee off on time, and there would be no one holding you up in front, no one pushing you from behind. You'd always have the right selection of club, be able to call every shot – and be right every time.

There'd be no cheating and the prizes would be things you'd never won before and really wanted – no more flipping crystal! There'd be a free supply of golf balls, but if it this was heaven you wouldn't need more than one. I'd also like a different coloured outfit for every day – a free wardrobe of clothes.

And there'd be ideal company. A heavenly four-ball would be Sevvy, Faldo and super coach David Leadbetter

– and all three would be asking my advice!

You would also have first crack at any new gadget that came out, and in the clubhouse you would be able to open a door and there would be a tract of land where all the lost balls land up. And a pond full of broken clubs and bags thrown in by frustrated golfers.

But at the end of the day it's only a game … Oh really? Every golfer knows you can get too obsessive with golf – yet they still persevere. Once the bug has bit (and we've come full circle now) golf becomes more important than anything (well nearly everything). People move house, change countries, retire early to play more. It's good for you, that's for sure. It may not cure all but it can help people who are stressed. Who knows, if Elvis had played golf, he might be alive today.

For a golfer it's heavenly to sit at a table and talk golf. It's a great thing to be able to talk with pride about other people's achievements. You can say, 'I was standing behind Nicklaus when he hit this ball …' and you actually have pride in some other guy playing better than you.

Golf is one of the few sports where there is pride from the people within and true sportsmanship among the players. Ask Christy O'Connor about when we did the business in the Ryder Cup that time and he hit a two-iron to the green and he will tell you the greatest help he had was from Sevvy. And that's great – to think that players, sometimes on opposite sides – will share with one another in competition. Try to get a hardbitten businessman to show you his tricks – no way!

When in the clubhouse, the only round they are interested in is theirs – they all want to tell you how *they* did, but in an ideal world they wouldn't want to know anything except how *you* did.

'How did you get on with Faldo?'

'Well, I put him right …'

— and heaven can wait

But coming back to golfing reality – if it really was no wind, no rain, it would be no fun, no challenge. So eventually the game has won anyway. It is the only game where you can't afford a rush of blood, the only game where you play yourself, where when you win the prize, only you know if you were pleased with the way you won it. That time when Sevvy hit the ball twice and only he knew and he declared it – nobody else would have known but he admitted it. Amazing that, but natural to a golfing great.

That, and the very many other things I have not the wit to write about, are the reasons why you and I play the great game.

One day it will all be worth it. That'll be the day when the phone rings and Faldo is at the other end saying, 'Tom, I need a partner this afternoon. How about it?'

Wow! What a moment that will be. And heaven can wait …